THREATENED MAMMALS OF INDIA

Ecology and Management

THREATENED MAMMALS OF INDIA

Ecology and Management

By
Goutam Kumar Saha, Ph.D.
Wildlife Biology Research Laboratory
Department of Zoology
University of Calcutta
&
Subhendu Mazumdar, M.Sc.
Department of Zoology
Shibpur Dinabundhoo College
University of Calcutta

2008

DAYA PUBLISHING HOUSE

Delhi - 110 035

ISBN10 81-7035-546-X
ISBN13 978-81-7035-546-5

Published by : **Daya Publishing House**
1123/74, Deva Ram Park
Tri Nagar, Delhi - 110 035
Phone: 27383999
Fax: (011) 23260116
e-mail : dayabooks@vsnl.com
website : www.dayabooks.com

Showroom : 4760-61/23, Ansari Road, Darya Ganj,
New Delhi - 110 002
Phone: 23245578, 23244987

Laser Typesetting : **Classic Computer Services**
Delhi - 110 035

Printed at : **Chawla Offset Printers**
Delhi - 110 052

PRINTED IN INDIA

Acknowledgements

Our special thanks are due to Mr. Rudra Prasad Das, Research Scholar, Calcutta University for his technical assistance in this endeavour. We extend our sincere thanks to Dr. D. Ghose, WWF-Sikkim Programme; Dr. K.Deuti, ZSI ; Dr. S.K.Tiwari, WTI; Mr. A. Basu Ray, Nature Mates and Mr. R. Das, CU for their kind permission to use some of their photographs in the present compilation. Mr. Abesh Kr. Sanyal of Calcutta University is acknowledged for the line drawings of the species provided in this book. We are thankful to the management and staff members of the Daya Publishing House, particularly Mr. Anil Kumar Mittal for his painstaking effort for this timely publication.

A good number of reference books on general wildlife as well as many websites have been consulted during the preparation of the manuscript which is gratefully acknowledged.

1. Alfred, J.R.B. and Chakraborty, S. 2002. *Endemic Mammals of India*. Zoological Survey of India, Kolkata, pp. 37.
2. Anon. 2003. *The Wildlife (Protection) Act, 1972–as amended upto 2003*. Nataraj Publishers, Dehradun, pp. 218.
3. Bedi, R. 1998. *Elephant–Lord of the Jungle*. National Book Trust, Delhi, pp. 103.
4. Kothari, A. 1997. *Understanding Biodiversity–Life, Sustainability and Equity*. Orient Longman Pvt. Limited, New Delhi, pp. 161.
5. Menon, V. 2003. *A Field Guide to Indian Mammals*. Dorling Kindersley (India) Pvt. Limited, Delhi, pp. 201.
6. Menon, V. and Kumar, A. 1998. *Wildlife Crime–an Enforcement Guide*. Wildlife Protection Society of India, New Delhi, pp. 109.
7. Monga, S. 2002. *Wildlife Reserves of India*. India Book House Pvt. Limited, Mumbai, pp. 151.

8. Nair, S.M. 2002. *Endangered Animals of India and their Conservation*. National Book Trust, Delhi, pp. 110.
9. National Biodiversity Authority. 2004. *The Biological Diversity Act, 2002 and Biological Diversity Rules, 2004*. National Biodiversity Authority, Chennai, pp. 57.
10. Prater, S.H. 1971. *The Book of Indian Animals*. Bombay Natural History Society, Mumbai, pp. 325.
11. Rangarajan, M. 2005. *India's Wildlife History–An Introduction*. Permanent Black, Delhi, pp. 135.
12. Roy Chowdhury, A. and Basu Roy, A. 2006. *A Conspectus of Mammals included under the Schedule I of the Wildlife (Protection) Act, 1972*. Wildlife Preservation (Eastern Region), Ministry of Environment and Forests, Government of India, pp. 42.
13. Saberwal, V., Rangarajan, M. and Kothari, A. 2001. *People, Parks and Wildlife–Towards Coexistence*. Orient Longman Pvt. Limited, New Delhi, pp. 143.
14. Sinha, B.C. 2001. *Book on State Animals, Birds, Trees and Flowers of India*. Wildlife Institute of India, Dehradun, pp. 39.
15. Tikader, B.K. 1983. *Threatened Animals of India*. Zoological Survey of India, Kolkata, pp. 307.
16. Tritsch, M.F. 2001. *Traveller's Guide–Wildlife of India*. Harper Collins Publishers Limited, pp. 192.
17. Zoological Survey of India. 1994. *The Red Data Book on Indian Animals. Part 1 : Vertebrata (Mammalia, Aves, Reptilia and Amphibia)*. Zoological Survey of India, Kolkata, pp. 534.

Photocredits

Mr. Abesh Kr. Sanyal

Malabar Large Spotted Civet, Lion-tailed Macaque, Hoolock Gibbon, Markhor, Gangetic Dolphin, Indian Giant Squirrel, Blackbuck, Urial or Shapu, Wild Yak, Asiatic Wild Ass, Himalayan Brown Bear, Golden Cat, Slender Loris.

Mr. Arjan Basu Roy

Asiatic Lion, Sloth Bear, Asiatic Wild Dog, Fishing Cat.

Dr. Dipankar Ghose

Clouded Leopard, Himalayan Musk Deer.

Dr. Kaushik Deuti

Pygmy Hog, Golden Langur, Greater One-horned Rhinoceros, Nilgiri Tahr.

Dr. P.K. Saikia

Hispid Hare.

Mr. Rudra Prasad Das

Brow-Antlered Deer, Capped Langur, Asiatic Wild Buffalo, Red Panda, Leopard, Swamp Deer.

Dr. Sandeep Kumar Tiwari

Tibetan Antelope, Bharal/Blue Sheep.

Mr. Subhendu Mazumdar

Asiatic Elephant, Tiger, Snow Leopard, Indian Bison.

Preamble

India occupies just 2.4 per cent of world's land area, yet it contributes to 8 per cent of the world's diversity of life-forms. It is considered to be one of the megadiversity countries of the world, harbouring a sizeable percentage of global floral and faunal wealth. India's biodiversity comprises of 11 per cent of plant species, 7.6 per cent of mammals, 12.6 per cent avian species, 6.2 per cent reptiles, 4.4 per cent amphibian and 11.7 per cent of the fish species of the world. This amazing biodiversity has traditionally been conserved in our country through Indian civilization. Conservation was an ardent article of faith in India as reflected in the daily lives of people and also in myths, folklores, rituals, religions, art and culture. However, population explosion as well as the spread of civilization across the world and at the same time ruthless overexploitation of nature and natural resources had taken its toll on the wildlife and its natural habitat throughout the globe. India is not an exception in this respect. Alteration of the environment, habitat destruction and fragmentation, pollution of land, air and water, hunting and poaching of animals are some of the major threats to the survival of several animal species. Infact it is the selfish interest of the human beings which have led them to overexploit the mother earth and as a consequence of this the human civilization itself is facing a tremendous pressure over its existence. In addition to that, rapid and unplanned urbanization, destruction of forests, construction of roads, railway tracts and dams, extension of agricultural activities including indiscriminate use of pesticides, atmospheric pollution, poaching and illegal trade of wildlife articles have resulted in the decline of several animal populations as well as altering their range of distribution in recent times.

Despite all odds, India is still one of the megadiversity countries in the world and can boast of the amazing diversity of its animal life. Scientific knowledge about the habits and habitats of the endangered animals is essential to adopt appropriate conservation strategies for their protection in the natural habitats. Hence, the need of the hour is a proper understanding of ecology and to identify the threats to the survival of the endangered wildlife of our country and to create awareness among the mass to prevent these life forms to peril in future.

Presently, there is a dearth of book dealing with the bioecology of the Indian threatened mammals. The present compilation includes the profile of thirty six species of mammals occurring in India which are getting top most importance from conservation point of view. This book deals with several aspects of morphology and behavioral biology of the threatened mammals of India. It not only describes the distribution of these animals in India, it also mentions the IUCN and local status as well as the WPA and CITES category of every species. This information helps to give a fair idea about the local and global status of that particular mammalian fauna and its legal status. This book documents the major threats to all the species and also specifies if any major conservation strategy has been adopted for a particular species that was considered to be in the verge of extinction. We hope that this book will serve as an important resource material for the students, academicians, naturalists, wildlife activists, policy makers as well as to the persons having interest in the field of wildlife.

Rathayatra

Goutam Kumar Saha

Subhendu Mazumdar

Contents

Conservation of Wildlife: Indian Perspective

The rich diversity of magnificent life forms was historically protected in this country through Indian civilization. The Indian tradition of love, respect and reverence for nature could be traced back to the Indus valley civilization. The seals of this period used to contain the inscriptions of rhinoceros, bull, elephant etc. that reflects their fascination for wildlife during this period. Historically, conservation was an ardent article of faith in India that was reflected in the daily lives of people. The conservation ethics date back in the 3rd century B.C. Emperor Ashoka enacted one of the earliest laws for conservation. The ethos of conservation was vividly reflected in several myths, folklores, art and culture and was quite prominent in the folk knowledge of our country. The tales of *Panchatantra* used to be the first lesson of conservation for any child in India.

Since independence, India has taken significant steps to conserve wildlife and its habitat through establishment of legislation, notifying protected areas and undertaking special conservation projects to protect the threatened animals of India. To conserve the flora and fauna, several laws have come to being. The State's commitment to protect the environment is mentioned in the Directive Principles of State Policy of the Indian Constitution. Article 48A of the Directive Principles states in clear and unambiguous terms that, "The State shall endeavor to protect and improve the environment and to safeguard the forests and wildlife of the country". It is the fundamental duty of every citizen of India "to protect and improve the natural environment, including forests, lakes, rivers and wildlife, and to have compassion for living creatures". Moreover, in 1972, Wildlife (Protection) Act was passed which was followed by Forest Protection Act in 1980. The Wildlife (Protection) Act, 1972, is a comprehensive central legislation affording legal measures for the protection of the wild animals. It not only provided countrywide legal protection to the endangered animals but also specified the provisions for the setting up of the protected areas, as well as regulation of trade and commerce in wild animals, animal parts, products and trophies. Three types of protected areas are notified *viz.*, National Park, Wildlife Sanctuaries and Reserve Forests. However, recently two more categories, Community Reserve and Conservation Reserve have been popularized.

In the late 1980s and early 1990s, the IUCN Commission on National Parks and Protected Areas (now known as the World Commission on Protected Areas–WCPA), reviewed these categories in the IVth World Parks Congress in Caracas and confirmed a number of changes and the IUCN General Assembly approved them in 1994. They were published as IUCN Guidelines in the same year.

The WCPA definition of a protected area and of the six associated management categories of protected areas are given below:

Protected areas may be defined as an area of land and/or sea especially dedicated to the protection and maintenance of biological diversity and of natural and associated cultural resources and managed through legal or other effective means.

§ **Category Ia:** ***Strict nature reserve/wilderness protection: protected area managed mainly for science or wilderness protection***–An area of land and/or sea possessing some outstanding or representative ecosystems, geological or physiological features and/or species, available primarily for scientific research and/or environmental monitoring.

§ **Category Ib:** ***Wilderness area: protected area managed mainly for wilderness protection***–Large area of unmodified or slightly modified land and/or sea, retaining its natural characteristics and influence, without permanent or significant habitation, which is protected and managed to preserve its natural condition.

§ **Category II:** ***National park: protected area managed mainly for ecosystem protection and recreation***–Natural area of land and/or sea designated to (a) protect the ecological integrity of one or more ecosystems for present and future generations, (b) exclude exploitation or occupation inimical to the purposes of designation of the area and (c) provide a foundation for spiritual, scientific, educational, recreational and visitor opportunities, all of which must be environmentally and culturally compatible.

§ **Category III:** ***Natural monument: protected area managed mainly for conservation of specific natural features***–Area containing specific natural or natural/cultural feature(s) of outstanding or unique value because of their inherent rarity, representativeness or aesthetic qualities or cultural significance.

§ **Category IV:** ***Habitat/Species Management Area: protected area managed mainly for conservation through management intervention***–Area of land and/or sea subject to active intervention for management purposes so as to ensure the maintenance of habitats to meet the requirements of specific species.

§ **Category V:** ***Protected Landscape/Seascape: protected area managed mainly for landscape/seascape conservation or recreation***–Area of land, with coast or sea as appropriate, where the interaction of people and nature over time has produced an area of distinct character with significant aesthetic, ecological and/or cultural value and often with high biological diversity. Safeguarding the integrity of this traditional interaction is vital to the protection, maintenance and evolution of such an area.

§ Category VI: ***Managed Resource Protected Area: protected area managed mainly for the sustainable use of natural resources***–Area containing predominantly unmodified natural systems, managed to ensure long-term protection and maintenance of biological diversity, while also providing a sustainable flow of natural products and services to meet community needs.

The Indian Board for Wildlife was constituted in 1952 to advise the Government on measures to be adopted for the conservation of our wildlife resources. Over the years, with the prime objective of preserving them as samples of interdependent ecological gene-pool combinations and a gene-bank capital, several national parks, wildlife sanctuaries and conservation reserves have been created in India in order to protect critical ecosystems and also to preserve the genetic resources of unquantifiable commercial and non-commercial values. The contributions of the Indian Board for Wildlife have been widely admired and respected. The country adopted the National Wildlife Action Plan in 2002 for meeting the new challenges in wildlife conservation. The National Board for Wildlife was constituted in September 2003 as a statutory authority, with full strength of law of the land behind it and is now entrusted with the responsibility for providing thrust to conservation activities.

According to the Protected Area database of the Wildlife Institute of India, at present there are 95 National Parks covering an area of 38,024.10 km^2 (1.16 per cent of geographical area of India), 500 Wildlife Sanctuaries covering an area of 117,913.45 km^2 (3.59 per cent of geographical area of India) and two Conservation Reserves covering an area of 40.50 km^2.

The concept of setting up of Biosphere Reserves evolved under the Man and Biosphere (MAB) programme of UNESCO. Biosphere Reserves are notified for conserving the biological diversity of a representative ecosystem including flora, fauna and microorganisms. These biosphere reserves provide facilities for education and awareness generation along with the scope of ecological research.

Besides notifying the Protected Areas, several conservation projects have been taken up for several endangered species to restore it from the verge of extinction. The major concept was that by protecting these keystones and umbrella species, the entire ecosystem would be protected. Gir Lion Sanctuary Project (1972), Project Tiger (1973), Himalayan Musk Deer Ecology and Conservation Project (1974), Manipur Brow-antlered Deer Project (1977), Project Hangul (1970), Crocodile Breeding Project (1975), Project Elephant (1971) are few success stories of the conservation projects in India. Years of protection and scientific management have saved many species that were in the verge of extinction. By notification of the protected areas, not only the species are saved, but natural habitats are also protected, thereby the entire ecosystem of the area was restored to health.

Besides, protecting the flora and fauna of our country through national legislation, India has played a significant role in the global scenario of wildlife conservation through international lobbying. India is a signatory to the Convention on International Trade in Endangered Species of Wild Fauna and Flora (CITES). This convention aims to prevent the international trade in wildlife articles. Illegal trade of wildlife articles in the present day has become the third biggest trade after ammunitions and narcotics. CITES is a major step towards wildlife conservation because it provides cooperation at the international level to curb this illegal trade.

However, the spread of civilization across the world and the progressive exploitation of nature had led to an adverse impact on the wildlife of our country. The disproportionately large human and livestock populations have made setting aside 4.7 per cent of country's geographical area under the protected area system increasingly difficult. The protected areas are all under tremendous stress caused by human interventions. Almost 40 per cent of these protected areas are subject to effects of traditional livestock grazing, fodder extraction, timber extraction, non-timber forest produce collection and more than 45 per cent have public thoroughfares dissecting them into smaller parts. Almost all have human habitations in or around them and a conflict of interest pervades the interface areas between the gene-pool reserves and the exploiters of the forest resources. These pressures are increasing with the rapid rise in the population of the country. People are not aware that more than 300 rivers originate in India's national parks and sanctuaries and many more do so in the forestlands outside these protected areas. Since the role of these natural life-sustaining systems is invisible to most people, our consumerist preoccupation for exploitation of forestlands and the life forms inhabiting them, for short-term gains, has created a barrier of indifference, resistance and even misdirected opposition against conservation of the nation's biodiversity. In the face of the fast-increasing human and livestock pressures on our country's woodlands and aquatic habitats and the undisguised hunger for land of various land-based activities, the protection of wildlife inside and outside our protected areas is progressively facing heavy odds and is fast becoming a difficult proposition. Indeed, we have lost some of the grandest species of flora and fauna forever, but we have also continued to protect a large number of species which otherwise would have been extinct by now.

The Asiatic Cheetah became extinct in India during the fifties due to excessive hunting and inbreeding. Hunting of animals, alteration of the environment, habitat destruction, pollution of the land, air and water, all these are the threats to survival for several animal species in recent times. Since the seventeenth century, about 120 species of mammals and 150 species of birds have become extinct. The present situation of several other mammals is quite gloomy. Population of Indian Wild Ass (*Equus onager*), One-horned Rhinoceros (*Rhinoceros unicornis*), Wild Buffalo (*Bubalus bubalis*), Swamp Deer (*Cervus duvaucelii*), Lion-tailed Macaque (*Macaca silenus*) and several other species number within few thousands. Wroughton's Freetailed Bat (*Otomops wroughtoni*) is only found in the Barapeda caves of Tamil Nadu and is considered as a critically endangered species.

Despite the continuing depletion of wildlife and the dwindling population of several species, India is still one of the megadiversity countries in the world and has got amazing diversity of its animal life. Scientific knowledge about the habits and habitats of the endangered animals is essential in evolving appropriate conservation strategies for their protection and to create public awareness. Hence, the need of the hour is a proper understanding of ecology and threats of the endangered wildlife of our country and to adopt proper and scientific conservation strategies to prevent these life forms to peril in future. In turn, we will thus ensure our own better survival in the lap of nature. However, the perception of conservation is changing these days. Conservation does not essentially mean just preservation of wildlife as it is, at the cost of man. Conservation involves sustainable utilization of natural resources and is based on ethical concern, aesthetic consideration, our need for sustenance and scientific understanding. According to the recent theory of conservation, local people should be involved for better management of an ecosystem through sustainable utilization of the bio-resources and fair and equitable benefit sharing.

Mammals–in a Nutshell

Mammals are the most charismatic of all fauna. These charismatic mega-fauna form a class that encompasses 4629 distinct species out of which around 400 species are found in India. The members of Class–Mammalia are diverse in nature ranging from enormous whales to tiny bats and rodents and are distributed in almost all habitable space of the world including underground, land, air and water. The characteristic features of all members belonging to this class are:

1. They are *endothermic* and *homoeothermic* (*i.e.* they produce heat from within their bodies and have the ability to regulate a constant internal temperature).
2. Presence of mammary glands (*i.e.* specialized sweat glands are located either on the chest or the abdomen) and female feed their offspring and young on the milk from their mammary glands till they are independent enough to procure their own food.
3. Presence of hair/fur (*i.e.* their skin is clothed with hair or fur)

About 210–280 million years ago, during Permian and early Triassic period, the sub-class of mammal-like reptiles called Synapsida dominated the reptilian community. However, in late Triassic, during the Mesozoic era (65–225 million years ago) the Synapsides were merely extinct because of the competitive superiority of the larger dinosaurs. Still, the Synapsides survived and the order–Therapsida, ancestors of present days mammals, evolved. Scientists now believe that all modern mammals orginated from a group that evolved from Synapsides called Cyanodonts, somewhat dog-like predators of middle and late Triassic. Approximately 200 million years ago first true mammals, known as Cyanodonts, evolved from the reptiles. However, the dinosaurs that dominated during that period marginalized Synapsids and Cyanodonts. Once the dinosaurs became extinct during geological strata line, called the Cretaceous-Tertiary, the mammals started to flourish and began to diversify. Mammals living in several strata evolved in different ways in response to their environment. Such evolution is the main cause of such a wide variation in the mammalian world.

IUCN Categories

Threatened mammals are those whose numbers are fewer than normal and whose habitats are constricted with several disturbances, or being fragmented or being destroyed altogether due to anthropogenic or natural cause. Animals are categorized into data deficient, least concern, near threatened, vulnerable, endangered, critically endangered, extinct in the wild and extinct depending upon their existing population size and degree of threats to their survival. The International Union for Conservation of Nature and Natural resources (IUCN) maintains record of animals that are known to be in danger in the "Red Data Book".

The Red List is a compilation of endangered wildlife species of a country whereas the Red Data Book provides data on population status of the species included in the Red List. Both the Red List and Red Data Book show the risk of extinction based on the biological data. They have no legal definition but serve as the scientific basis for the promotion of endangered wildlife conservation. The first Red Data Book of animals, compiled in 1991 by the Environment Agency, needed a periodical revision as a result of changes in wildlife distribution and habitat. In addition, IUCN adopted a revised set of Red List Categories in 1994. Because of these two reasons, the Environment Agency has been revising, since 1995, the Red List and Red Data Book by setting up a group of specialists in mammals, birds, amphibians, reptiles and so on. In December 1994, IUCN adopted a revised set of Red List Categories. The revision had been prepared, since 1989, mainly by the IUCN Species Survival Commission (SSC). The text below contains the definitions of the categories as given in the IUCN Red Data Book:

EXTINCT (EX)

A taxon is Extinct when exhaustive surveys in known and/or expected habitat, at appropriate times (diurnal, seasonal, annual), throughout the historic range of the species over a time frame appropriate to the taxon's life-cycle and life form reveals that there is no reasonable doubt that the last individual has died and no longer exist in captivity as well as in the wild.

EXTINCT IN THE WILD (EW)

A taxon is Extinct in the Wild when exhaustive surveys for over a time frame appropriate to the taxon's life cycle and life form in the known and/or expected habitat, at appropriate times (diurnal, seasonal, annual), throughout the historic range of the species have failed to record an individual and it is known only to survive in cultivation, in captivity or as a naturalized population (or populations) well outside the past range.

CRITICALLY ENDANGERED (CR)

A taxon is Critically Endangered when the best available evidence indicates that it meets any of the following criteria and it is therefore considered to be facing a very high risk of extinction in the wild:

1. An observed, estimated, inferred or suspected population size reduction of $\geq$ 90 per cent over the last 10 years or three generations, whichever is the longer, where the causes of the reduction are clearly reversible AND understood AND ceased and it is therefore considered to be facing an extremely high risk of extinction in the wild. OR
2. Quantitative analysis showing the probability of extinction in the wild is at least 50 per cent within 10 years or three generations, whichever is the longer (up to a maximum of 100 years). OR
3. Extent of occurrence estimated to be less than 100 km^2, and estimates indicating severely fragmented habitat or known to exist at only a single location. OR
4. Continuing decline and extreme fluctuations of the species is observed, inferred or projected in extent of occurrence, area of occupancy, number of locations or subpopulations and number of mature individuals.

ENDANGERED (EN)

A taxon is Endangered when the best available evidence indicates that it meets any of the following criteria and it is therefore considered to be facing a very high risk of extinction in the wild:

1. An observed, estimated, inferred or suspected population size reduction of $\geq$70 per cent over the last 10 years or three generations, whichever is the longer, where the causes of the reduction are clearly reversible AND understood AND ceased and it is therefore considered to be facing an extremely high risk of extinction in the wild. OR
2. Quantitative analysis showing the probability of extinction in the wild is at least 20 per cent within 20 years or five generations, whichever is the longer (up to a maximum of 100 years). OR
3. Extent of occurrence estimated to be less than 5000 km^2, and estimates indicating severely fragmented habitat or known to exist in not more than five locations. OR

4. Continuing decline and extreme fluctuations of the species is observed, inferred or projected in extent of occurrence, area of occupancy, number of locations or subpopulations and number of mature individuals.

VULNERABLE (VU)

A taxon is vulnerable when the best available evidence indicates that it meets any of the following criteria and it is therefore considered to be facing a very high risk of extinction in the wild:

1. An observed, estimated, inferred or suspected population size reduction of $\geq$ 50 per cent over the last 10 years or three generations, whichever is the longer, where the causes of the reduction are clearly reversible AND understood AND ceased and it is therefore considered to be facing an extremely high risk of extinction in the wild. OR
2. Quantitative analysis showing the probability of extinction in the wild is at least 10 per cent within 100 years. OR
3. Extent of occurrence estimated to be less than 20,000 km^2, or area of occupancy estimated to be less than 2000 km^2, and estimates indicating severely fragmented habitat or known to exist in not more than ten locations. OR
4. Continuing decline and extreme fluctuations of the species is observed, inferred or projected in extent of occurrence, area of occupancy, number of locations or subpopulations and number of mature individuals.

NEAR THREATENED (NT)

A taxon is Near Threatened when it has been evaluated but does not qualify for Critically Endangered, Endangered or Vulnerable (according to the Red Data Book criteria for the same) at present, but is close to qualifying for or is likely to qualify for a threatened category in the near future.

LEAST CONCERN (LC)

A taxon is Least Concern when it has been evaluated and does not qualify for Critically Endangered, Endangered, Vulnerable or Near Threatened (according to the Red Data Book criteria for the same) at present as well as estimated to have a good chance to perpetuate in future. Widespread and abundant taxa are included in this category.

DATA DEFICIENT (DD)

A taxon is Data Deficient when there is inadequate information to make a direct, or indirect, assessment of its risk of extinction based on its distribution and/or population status. A taxon in this category may be well studied, and its biology is well known, but appropriate data on abundance and/or distribution are lacking. Data Deficient is therefore not a category of threat. Listing of taxa in this category indicates that more information is required and acknowledges the possibility that future research will show that threatened classification is appropriate. It is important to make positive use of whatever data are available. In many cases great care should be exercised in choosing between DD and a threatened status. If the range of a taxon is suspected to be relatively circumscribed, and a considerable period of time has elapsed since the last record of the taxon, threatened status may well be justified.

NOT EVALUATED (NE)

A taxon is Not Evaluated when it is has not yet been evaluated against the criteria.

Note: Definitions abridged from the IUCN Red List Categories (1994), IUCN.

Threatened Mammals of India

There are nearly 372 species of mammals found in India including following 84 species listed in threatened categories (IUCN Red List of Threatened Animals).

Threatened Mammals of India

Scientific Name	*Common Name*	*IUCN Category*
Ailurus fulgens	RED PANDA	EN
Alticola montosa	CENTRAL KASHMIR VOLE	VU
Balaenoptera borealis	COALFISH WHALE	EN
Balaenoptera musculus	BLUE WHALE	EN
Balaenoptera physalus	FIN-BACKED WHALE	EN
Biswamoyopterus biswasi	NAMDAPHA FLYING SQUIRREL	CR
Bos frontalis	GAUR or INDIAN BISON	VU
Bos grunniens	WILD YAK	VU
Bubalus bubalis	ASIATIC WILD BUFFALO	EN
Budorcas taxicolor	TAKIN	VU
Bunopithecus hoolock	HOOLOCK GIBBON	EN
Callosciurus pygerythrus	IRRAWADDY SQUIRREL	VU
Capra aegagrus	WILD GOAT	VU
Capra falconeri	MARKHOR	EN
Capricornis sumatraensis	SEROW	VU
Caprolagus hispidus	HISPID HARE	EN
Catopuma temminckii	GOLDEN CAT	VU
Cervus duvaucelii	SWAMP DEER	VU
Cervus eldii	BROW-ANTLERED DEER	VU

Contd...

Contd...

Scientific Name	Common Name	IUCN Category
Cremnomys elvira	ELVIRA RAT	VU
Crocidura hispida	ANDAMAN SPINY SHREW	EN
Crocidura pergrisea	PALE GREY SHREW	VU
Cuon alpinus	ASIATIC WILD DOG or DHOLE	EN
Dugong dugon	DUGONG or SEA COW	VU
Elephas maximus	ASIAN ELEPHANT	EN
Equus hemionus	ASIATIC WILD ASS	VU
Eupetaurus cinereus	WOOLLY FLYING SQUIRREL	EN
Hemiechinus nudiventris	BARE-BELLIED HEDGEHOG	VU
Hemitragus hylocrius	NILGIRI TAHR	EN
Hemitragus jemlahicus	HIMALAYAN TAHR	VU
Herpestes palustris	MARSH MONGOOSE	EN
Hipposideros durgadasi	KHAJURIA'S LEAF-NOSED BAT	EN
Hipposideros hypophyllus	KOLAR LEAF-NOSED BAT	EN
Hylopetes alboniger	PARTICOLORED FLYING SQUIRREL	EN
Hystrix brachyura	MALAYAN PORCUPINE	VU
Latidens salimalii	SALIM ALI'S FRUIT BAT	EN
Lutrogale perspicillata	SMOOTH-COATED OTTER	VU
Macaca arctoides	STUMP-TAILED MACAQUE	VU
Macaca assamensis	ASSAMESE MACAQUE	VU
Macaca silenus	LION-TAILED MACAQUE	EN
Martes gwatkinsii	NILGIRI MARTEN	VU
Megaptera novaeangliae	HUMPBACK WHALE	VU
Melursus ursinus	SLOTH BEAR	VU
Millardia kondana	KONDANA SOFT-FURRED RAT	EN
Murina grisea	PETER'S TUBE-NOSED BAT	CR
Mus famulus	SERVANT MOUSE	EN
Mustela strigidorsa	BACK-STRIPED WEASEL	VU
Myotis longipes	KASHMIR CAVE BAT	VU
Myotis sicarius	MANDELLI'S MOUSE-EARED BAT	VU
Naemorhedus baileyi	RED GORAL	VU
Neofelis nebulosa	CLOUDED LEOPARD	VU
Otomops wroughtoni	WROUGHTON'S FREE-TAILED BAT	CR
Ovis ammon	ARGALI	VU
Ovis orientalis	URIAL	VU
Panthera tigris	TIGER	EN

Contd...

Contd...

Scientific Name	Common Name	IUCN Category
Pantholops hodgsonii	TIBETAN ANTELOPE or CHIRU	EN
Paradoxurus jerdoni	BROWN PALM CIVET	VU
Pardofelis marmorata	MARBLED CAT	VU
Physeter macrocephalus	SPERM WHALE	VU
Platanista gangetica	GANGETIC RIVER DOLPHIN	EN
Prionailurus rubiginosus	RUSTY-SPOTTED CAT	VU
Prionailurus viverrinus	FISHING CAT	VU
Pteropus faunulus	NICOBAR FLYING FOX	EN
Rattus burrus	NONSENSE RAT	VU
Rattus palmarum	PALM RAT	VU
Rattus ranjiniae	KERALA RAT	VU
Rattus sikkimensis	SIKKIM RAT	VU
Rattus stoicus	ANDAMAN RAT	VU
Ratufa indica	INDIAN GIANT SQUIRREL	VU
Ratufa macroura	GRIZZLED GIANT SQUIRREL	VU
Rhinoceros unicornis	GREATER ONE-HORNED RHINOCEROS	EN
Rhinolophus cognatus	ANDAMAN HORSESHOE BAT	VU
Rhinolophus mitratus	MITRED HORSESHOE BAT	VU
Semnopithecus johnii	NILGIRI LANGUR	VU
Suncus dayi	DAY'S SHREW	VU
Suncus montanus	SRI LANKA HIGHLAND SHREW	VU
Sus salvanius	PYGMY HOG	CR
Tetracerus quadricornis	FOUR-HORNED ANTELOPE	VU
Trachypithecus geei	GOLDEN LANGUR	EN
Trachypithecus pileatus	CAPPED LANGUR	EN
Tupaia nicobarica	NICOBAR TREE SHREW	EN
Uncia uncia	OUNCE or SNOW LEOPARD	EN
Ursus thibetanus	HIMALAYAN BLACK BEAR	VU
Viverra civettina	MALABAR LARGE-SPOTTED CIVET	CR

CR: Critically Endangered; EN: Endangered; VU: Vulnerable.

Source: www.iucnredlist.org.

In India, the Wildlife (Protection) Act, 1972 provides four schedules, categorizing the fauna of India based on their conservation status. Schedule – I lists the rare and endangered species that are provided with the highest legal protection within the country. An offence, involving Schedule – I species, on conviction, is punishable under Section – 51 of WPA, 1972 with imprisonment for a term which shall not be less than three years but may extend to seven years and also with fine which shall not be less than ten thousand rupees. Most of the threatened mammals of India have been incorporated in this Schedule – I of Wildlife (Protection) Act, 1972, thereby giving them a countrywide legal protection from poaching and illegal destruction of these animals.

CRITICALLY ENDANGERED

PYGMY HOG

Order: Artiodactyla

Family: Suidae

***Sus salvanius* (Hodgson)**

Common Name

Nal gahori, Takori borah (Assamese), *Sano Banel* (Nepalese).

Present Status

Wildlife (Protection) Act, 1972	Schedule–I
IUCN	Critically Endangered
CITES	Appendix–I
Local Status	Rare

Distribution

Worldwide Distribution

The distribution of Pygmy Hog is restricted to the Terai region of India, Nepal and Bhutan.

Distribution in India

In India, the Pygmy Hog is restricted to the plains of Brahmaputra River in south and south-east Assam. Some isolated populations are also found in Manas Biosphere Reserve and Barnadi Wildlife Sanctuary in north-west Assam.

Habitat

Pygmy Hog prefers dense, tall riverine grasslands and forest habitat.

Distinctive Characters

Pygmy Hog is the world's smallest pig having a total body length of about 50-70 cm and shoulder height of 25 cm. Male Pygmy Hogs weigh about 8-9 kg, females are smaller than males. Adult Pygmy Hogs are gray-brown to black in appearance and have no crest on back. The youngs are lighter in appearance and with reddish stripes. Ears are very small and characteristically very short tail, which is sometimes not visible. The male Hog generally possesses small tusks.

Behavioural Biology

Pygmy Hogs groom each other and make soft grunting sound at the time of foraging, which keep them together. Both the sexes build unique nests by scraping and digging the forest floor in a very characteristic manner and also use piles of grass and other vegetation to lay in the floor of the burrow. Pygmy Hog generally use this burrows for sleeping at night. They are nocturnal in habit. Their sense of smell is acute, while the sighting and hearing are moderately developed.

Feeding Behaviour

The Pygmy Hogs are omnivorous in nature and feeds on roots, tubers, crops and other vegetable matters, as well as, insects and other invertebrates. They feed during early in the morning and late in the evening.

Reproductive Behaviour

Reproduction is highly seasonal and the birth takes place during the dry months or with the onset of monsoon (April and May). Gestation period is about 100 days. The females generally give birth to 2–6 youngs. They can survive upto 10–12 years in the wild.

Social Organization

The Pygmy Hog is non-territorial and found to live in small family groups consisting of 4–5 individuals, which sometimes may reach upto 20 individuals. Generally one or more adult females are accompanied by juveniles. Adult males remain solitary, but join with females or family groups during rut. The home range of Pygmy Hog extends upto 25 hectares.

Threats to Survival

1. Habitat loss due to human settlement, agricultural encroachment, overgrazing by domestic livestock, commercial forestry etc.
2. The grassland habitat, which they prefer, is periodically burned in dry months of the year.
3. Poaching.

Conservation Measures

According to IUCN, Pygmy Hog is designated as Critically Endangered, where as its local status is Rare and it is placed in the Schedule–I of Wildlife (Protection) Act, 1972 providing the animal a nationwide legal protection. Most of the areas of their concentration have been declared as conservation areas. Being in the Appendix–I of CITES, prevents any part of it from being used in international trade.

Preservation of its habitat in the north and northeastern India, particularly in Assam need to be prioritized and field data should be collected to understand the present population status and distribution of Pygmy Hog and if found necessary new sanctuaries for its conservation need to be established. Experts had suggested for establishing an enclosure at Manas Biosphere Reserve where a good number of Pygmy Hog could be protected, studied and bred. The transfer of a breeding nucleus to a research institute or a Zoological Garden in Europe and North America has also been suggested.

ASIATIC LION

Order: Carnivora

Family: Felidae

***Panthera leo persica* (Meyer)**

Common Name

Sher, Sher babar, Singh (Hindi); *Sinha* (Marathi); *Untia bagh* (Gujrati); *Sawach* (Kathiawari); *Simham* (Malayali); *Singham* (Tamil); *Singha* (Bengali)

Present Status

Wildlife (Protection) Act, 1972	Schedule–I
IUCN	Critically Endangered
CITES	Appendix–I
Local Status	Locally common

Distribution

Worldwide Distribution

Though Asiatic Lion was previously found in Iran and Iraq, however, it is presently found only in India.

Distribution in India

In India, single population is found only in the Gir National Park of Gujarat.

Habitat

Asiatic Lion inhabits the scrub and dry, deciduous forests (teak forest). Presently Asiatic Lion lives in the rugged terrain of Gir National Park composed mainly of

Teak, Palas, Jambul, Ber and patches of bamboo grooves with undergrowth of thorny shrubs and bushes.

Distinctive Characters

Asiatic Lion is about 2.75 meter in length and weighs between 150–250 kg with a shoulder height of about 1–1.23 meter. Both male and female bear pale yellowish or sandy gray coat without any marking. The cubs are marked with spots and stripes. Both male and female of Asiatic Lions have a longitudinal fold of skin in belly and a long naked tail with a tuft of hair at the tip.

The sexual dimorphism is very distinct in Asiatic Lion. The lion bears a scanty mane, which is absent in the lioness. The body size of the males is much bigger than the females. Presence of scrotal sacs in the males is another distinguishing character. During breeding season, conspicuous mammary gland is evident in the females. The mammary gland in found along the ventro-lateral side of the body from the axilla to the groin of the lioness. Lions have a potential life span of 20–30 years, but they rarely reach this age in the wild.

Behavioural Biology

Asiatic Lions are predatory in nature and generally nocturnal in habit. They rest during daytime under the shade of the trees and at dusk go in search of food. Their roars are heard throughout the night, most noticeably during dusk and dawn. Asiatic Lion generally do not attack human unless it is threatened, bothered, wounded or diseased. They have a strongly developed sense of hearing.

Lion cubs are born blind and their dentition appears after 15 days. During this period they are very much vulnerable and fall prey to Leopard and other predators. During this time, their mother carries them in her mouth and cleans by licking with her tongue. Lactation continues for about 5–5.5 months and after that they are being fed with meat. Lioness trains its cubs all the hunting strategies so that they can hunt by their own in future. The male parent stays with the family and provides protection to the youngs. The males mark their territory by spraying urine into the tree trunks and several other prominent stationary posts.

Feeding Behaviour

The Asiatic Lion in the wild mainly feed on the cattle and game animals present inside the Gir National Park. In the forest they stalk their prey by making a short, high-speed chase with a speed up to 80 km per hour. The prey is grabbed with one paw on the back and the other on the flank or chest to drag it down. Then they bite the throat of its prey until the victim dies of suffocation. The lionesses do most of the hunting in a lion pride and the males join the group once the kill is made. They only feed on the meat without crushing the bones or picking them clean, usually leaving enough for the scavengers. Lions generally eat until they are fully satiated and after having a full-meal they may not hunt for several days and completely ignore the presence of prey in their vicinity. Amount of food consumed by a full-grown Asiatic Lion is about 10–12 kg daily.

Reproductive Behaviour

Asiatic Lions are polyestrous animals and do not possess a particular breeding season. When a female is sexually mature, it pairs with a sexually mature male and mate. The peak mating season is between October and November and the youngs are produced between January and February. The period of gestation is about 116 days and youngs are produced at an interval of 18–24 months. The litter number varies from normally 2 to as many as 5 at times. Generally, the females become sexually mature within 2–3 years whereas a male attains maturity at around five years of age. In nature, the males follow the female in heat and there is severe competition among the males for mate selection.

Social Organization

Lions are most sociable among the cats. They live in loosely knit groups that are known as 'prides', which typically consists of 2–5 females, usually related to one another and their young. Adult males become temporary members of the pride living for few months to years. There are fierce battles among the males to take possession of a pride and the winner dominates the entire pride and also gets the privilege to mate with any and every receptive female of that pride. When this dominant male becomes old or shows signs of weakness, he is replaced forcefully by a younger and more vigorous one.

Threats to Survival

Single population of Asiatic Lion is presently found in Gujarat and that is also threatened by several natural and anthropogenic factors.

1. Destruction of the habitats of these animals due to extension of human settlements and agricultural lands, construction of roads and illegal logging had presently restricted them to a single population.
2. Poaching of the animals for their hide and skin. Previously Asiatic Lion was also hunted for sport in large number by the *maharajas* to collect the trophy for pride.
3. Several bacterial, viral and helminthic diseases. Bacterial disease like Feline infectious anaemia is caused by *Hemobartenella felis* and Plague is caused by *Yersinia pestis*. Viral diseases caused by Feline Parvo virus and Feline Herpes virus–I leading to Kerato conjunctivitis affect the cubs. Helminthes such as Round worm (*Ancylostoma braziliensis*) and Tape worm (*Dipylidium sp.*) also infect the cubs and the adults.
4. As only single population of Asiatic Lion is present in India, therefore high amount of inbreeding threatens its survival.
5. Natural calamities like drought, flood and fire also affect lion population.

Conservation Measures

Asiatic Lions are confined to one population in the Gir National Park of India and this subspecies is listed as Critically Endangered on the IUCN Red List and is on Appendix–I of CITES. Earlier the population of Asiatic Lion consisted of less than

200 mature individuals, however, presently their number has increased. To safeguard the survival of this subspecies, presently a population of Asiatic Lion is being considered to be reintroduced to the Palpur-Kuno Wildlife Sanctuary in northern Madhya Pradesh. Threats to the Gir forest population include human-animal conflict in the form of cattle killing by the lions and habitat degradation through cattle grazing and other non-forest activities by the villagers present inside the boundary of the protected area.

MALABAR LARGE-SPOTTED CIVET

Order: Carnivora

Family: Viverridae

***Viverra civettina* (Blyth)**

Common Name

Jawad, Malabar veruke (Malayam), *Mangala Kutri, Jawadiya* (Kannada)

Present Status

Wildlife (Protection) Act, 1972	Schedule–I
IUCN	Critically Endangered
CITES	Appendix–III
Local Status	Rare

Distribution

Worldwide Distribution

Malabar Large-spotted Civets are not found in any other part of the world except India. However, there are reports of their presence in Sri Lanka.

Distribution in India

In India, this civet is found in the coastal districts of Malabar and Travancore. Probably, it is the most endangered mammal living in India and is presently in the verge of extinction. Only a small isolated population of Malabar Large-spotted Civet still survives in less disturbed areas of south Malabar.

Habitat

Their favourite habitat is the tropical rain forests in the Western Ghats of south-west India. They generally prefers wooded plains and adjoining hill slopes. But due to human settlements and activities, natural forests have almost completely disappeared in the entire stretch of the coastal Western Ghats. The present vegetation consists mostly of cashew plantations, which are least disturbed and provide important cover to these civets.

Distinctive Characters

Malabar Large-spotted Civet's large size and the dark erectile crest of hair that runs down its spine (the dark band runs through to the tip of the tail) make it distinguishable from the Small Indian Civets. The underside of the tail has five alternate bands of black and white. The body colour is grey with randomly distributed black spots. Total body length, including tail, is about 125 cm. and its weight is approximately 8–9 kg.

Behavioural Biology

It is typically a ground dwelling animal and it has never been found on trees and possibly forages almost entirely on the ground. Generally they stay in dense cover during daytime and come out into the open at night for hunting.

Feeding Behaviour

It is an omnivore and its diet includes small animals, eggs, frogs, crabs and even insects. They also take vegetables, berries, fruits etc. depending upon the season.

Reproductive Behaviour

Very little is known about its breeding behaviour. Birth generally takes place during May and June. Females usually give birth to 2–4 youngs.

Social Organization

Malabar Large-spotted Civets are solitary in nature and show aggression towards the members of their own species.

Threats to Survival

1. Habitat loss due to extensive deforestation.
2. Probably most of the surviving Malabar Large-spotted Civet population inhabits in cashew plantations, but now is in danger as cashew plantations are being replaced by rubber plantations.
3. Malabar Large-spotted Civet is not a game animal, but has been persecuted for raiding poultry.
4. There is no selective hunting but is captured and killed when encountered.

Conservation Measures

According to IUCN, Malabar Large-spotted Civet is designated as Critically Endangered, its local status is Rare and it is placed in the Schedule–I of Wildlife

(Protection) Act, 1972, providing the animal a nationwide legal protection. Most of the areas of their concentration have been declared as conservation areas. It has been also included in Appendix–III of CITES.

The status survey along the Western Ghats, particularly within the listed conservation areas, as well as detailed ecological study of the areas where this species is still reported to be occuring, is necessary to identify the causes of decline and to suggest conservation measures to prevent its further decline. The remnant populations are found in isolated habitats where immediate protection measures are unlikely to succeed. Experts suggested that attention should be given to capture these specimens, prepare a founder stock and to initiate a captive breeding programme. The species should be enlisted in Appendix–I of CITES to curb international trade, if any.

ENDANGERED

LION-TAILED MACAQUE

Order: Primate

Family: Cercopithecidae

Macaca silenus **(Linnaeus)**

Common Name

Arakkan, Karungkorungoo (Tamil), *Singalika* (Kannada), *Nella Manthi, Singhawalan, Chingala, Neelam* (Malayam), *Siah Bandar* (Hindi)

Present Status

Wildlife (Protection) Act, 1972	Schedule–I
IUCN	Endangered
CITES	Appendix–I
Local Status	Rare

Distribution

Worldwide Distribution

Lion-tailed Macaques are found both in India and Sri Lanka.

Distribution in India

Lion-tailed Macaque is not very common. It is found in the southern parts of India, generally in the Western Ghats; also in some scattered locations in Karnataka, Kerala and Tamil Nadu (Kanyakumari district). Its distribution ranges from the northern Kanara district of Karnataka in the north to the Ashambu Hills near the tip of the Indian subcontinent in the south. The maximum concentration of this macaque has been noticed at Silent Valley National Park (Kerala), Kalakkad and Annamalai Wildlife Sanctuary (Tamil Nadu) within its range.

Habitat

Lion-tailed Macaque is found in tropical evergreen and semi-evergreen forest belt between 610 and 1070 m above the sea level. Apparently they do not travel through plantations or use them as habitat.

Distinctive Characters

Lion-tailed Macaque can be distinguished from all other species of macaques by its long, dark-gray or brownish-grey coloured facial mane and a much shorter tufted tail that looks more or less similar to a lion's tail. Body colour of both male and female is glossy black. The head and body length of Lion-tailed Macaque is 45–60 cm, tail measuring about 25–40 cm. and weight is about 7–15 kg. Females appear slightly smaller than males in size.

Behavioural Biology

Lion-tailed Macaque is mainly arboreal, although it does occasionally descend to the ground. Like all other macaques they are primarily diurnal in habit. Generally they move through the treetops very slowly.

Feeding Behaviour

Lion-tailed Macaque is omnivorous in nature.

Reproductive Behaviour

Lion-tailed Macaque generally mates in the winter months. Gestation period is about 5.5 months. During August-September, the female gives birth to single young. The females become sexually mature at the age of 5 years, while in case of male it is 8 years.

Social Organization

Like other macaques, they are gregarious in nature. Troops of Lion-tailed Macaques may consist of 4–34 individuals, including 1–3 adult males.

Threats to Survival

1. Habitat loss due to the spread of agricultural lands for teak, coffee, tea and other plantations.
2. The trade of live Lion-tailed Macaque to zoos and research laboratories were formerly very prevalent. However, legislation has probably limited this practice in most recent years.

3. Lion-tailed Macaque's meat and bones are valued for use in traditional oriental medicine.

Conservation Measures

According to IUCN Lion-tailed Macaque is designated as Endangered, its local status is Rare and it is placed in the Schedule–I of Wildlife (Protection) Act, 1972 providing the animal a nationwide legal protection. Most of the areas of their concentration have been declared as conservation areas. Being in the Appendix–I of CITES, prevents any part of it from being used in international trade. Karanth (1984) has suggested that Kudremukh, Brahmagiri, Mukambika, Talkavere, Pushpagiri, Someshwara and Saravathi forest areas of Karnataka to be declared as conservation areas, the first three as Biosphere Reserves and the latter four as sanctuaries for the conservation of Lion-tailed Macaques.

GOLDEN LANGUR

Order: Primate

Family: Cercopithecidae

Trachypithecus geei
(Khajuria)

Common Name

Sonali bandar (Assamese); *Sugrib* (Bhotia); *Makre gophur* (Bodo)

Present Status

Wildlife (Protection) Act, 1972	Schedule–I
IUCN	Endangered
CITES	Appendix–I
Local Status	Uncommon

Distribution

Worldwide Distribution

Golden Langurs are distributed in the forests of India and Bhutan.

Distribution in India

This beautiful primate is found in the forests between river Manas and river Sankosh in Kokrajhar, Bongaigaon and Dhubri districts of Assam up to an altitude of 2400 m.

Habitat

Golden Langurs inhabit moist evergreen and tropical deciduous forests as well as some riverine areas and savannas. They are arboreal and prefer the upper canopy level of subtropical forests in the south and in more temperate forests in the north. The elevation within their distribution range varies greatly, ranging from sea level to 3000 m at the foothills.

Distinctive Characters

This is one of the most beautiful langurs found in India. The coat varies from deep cream to golden in colour with tinges of red on the flanks where the hairs are longer, darker and almost red. It has a black face with long cheek whiskers and a cap of hair on their head. Golden Langur also has a distinctive long, tasseled tail. Their coat colour is lighter during summer and takes a darker hue during winter season. Youngs and females appear silvery white to light golden yellow in colour. Body length of Golden Langur varies from 50–60 cm and weighs 9.5–11 kg.

Behavioural Biology

Golden Langur is a very shy animal and generally avoids humans. They are diurnal in nature and most áctive in early morning and afternoon. They spend most of their time on the tree and rarely come down to drink.

Feeding Behaviour

Golden Langurs are exclusively vegetarian in nature, hence also known as Leaf Monkey. They are both folivores and frugivores. They prefer to eat young leaves. Their diet also consist of ripe and unripe fruits, young and mature leaves, leaf buds, flower buds, seeds, twigs and flowers.

Reproductive Behaviour

Very little is known about the breeding behaviour of Golden Langur. It has been observed that birth occur almost year-round, mainly during July-August. Generally they give birth to a single offspring at a time.

Social Organization

Golden Langurs tend to live in troops that ranges anywhere from 4-40 members, with an average troop size of eight. Each troop consists of a male and one or more females and several sub-adults. Social grooming is very common, where mothers and other females take care of the youngs.

Threats to Survival

1. Localized habitat and loss of habitat due to deforestation.
2. Increasing Langur-Human conflict due to destruction of their habitat.
3. Poaching for their hide, skin and meat.

Conservation Measures

Golden Langur is placed in the Schedule–I of Wildlife (Protection) Act, 1972, thus providing a countrywide legal protection. Several protected areas have been declared in its distribution range to protect the animal from poaching. In India, this animal is best seen at the Chakrashila Wildlife Sanctuary and Manas National Park in Assam. The IUCN status of Golden Langur is Endangered.

The main cause of the decline of the Golden Langur is because of their localized habitat and the rapid loss of this habitat due to deforestation. Although the forests are supposedly protected, until recently their protection was not strictly enforced and it is estimated that approximately 50 per cent of their habitat has lost from India during last 10 to 12 years. Surveys revealed that in 1998, approximately 4,500 Golden Langurs remained in both Assam and Bhutan in approximately 95 square km of their habitat which is protected by the two Wildlife Sanctuaries in Assam–the Manas Wildlife Sanctuary and Chakrasilla Wildlife Sanctuary. In spite of the need for immediate action, it was reported that the area, the species inhabited, shrunk again from 1998 to 2002. Although at current rates of decline, the survival of these animals seems bleak, there have been some efforts to save them. Most of their distribution areas in Bhutan is part of four different wildlife reserves and national parks that have been set up for the conservation of this species namely–The Royal Manas National Park, Black Mountain National Park, Trumsingla Wildlife Sanctuary and Phipsoo Wildlife Sanctuary and are home to more than half of the total number of Golden Langurs living today. Certain conservation organizations, along with the Indo-US Primate Project are working together to assure the future of this species. Aside from protecting the forest reserves, they are also working with local residents to rebuild the forests that were once the home of the Golden Langurs.

CAPPED LANGUR

Order: Primate

Family: Cercopithecidae

***Trachypithecus pileatus* (Blyth)**

Common Name

Tupimuria (Assamese); *Rangol* (Garo); *Tongo* (Khasi); *Goliga makhre* (Bodo); *Bilaspuri* (Manipuri); *Ngau* (Mizo)

Present Status

Wildlife (Protection) Act, 1972	Schedule–I
IUCN	Endangered
CITES	Appendix–I
Local Status	Locally common

Distribution

Worldwide Distribution

Capped Langur is found in India, Bangladesh and upper Myanmar.

Distribution in India

In India, this monkey is distributed throughout northeast India upto an altitude of 2000 m. Four races, distinctive in colour, inhabit hill ranges of Assam and other states of northeastern India. The fifth race is present in Myanmar.

Habitat

Capped Langur is present in the dense deciduous and evergreen forest. They live in the dense forests that cover the hills of the states of northeast India.

Distinctive Characters

This is the common forest monkey of northeast India and has distinct races with varying colouration. A distinct cap of dark coloured, erect, long and backwardly directed course hair is present. The general coat colour of all the races varies from golden–cream to grey in the dorsal surface and fulvous ventral surface with a black tipped tail. The newborn monkeys are golden, golden red and creamy white in appearance. The average body size of the male varies from 60–70 cm, weighing about 10–15 kg. The tail is 75–100 cm long. Females are smaller and lighter. The cheeks of Capped Langur have large tufts of pale hair.

Behavioural Biology

Capped Langurs are arboreal in nature and stay exclusively on the trees and hardly come down to the ground. They take most of the water from dew or rain-drenched leaves. They are very shy and wary forest dwellers and when threatened, they quickly escape or hide them behind the foliages. Capped Langurs make a sharp guttural bark as alarm call and other vocal sounds include squealing. They live a diurnal mode of life.

Feeding Behaviour

Capped Langurs are strictly vegetarian in nature. They feed on fruit, flower and leaves.

Reproductive Behaviour

They are typical winter-breeder and during cold weather their breeding activity is specially marked. However, the period of gestation is not known.

Social Organization

Very little is known about the social life of Capped Langur. They live in troops. During winter, these troops consist of a male and a harem of 3–4 females and their immature youngs. Most of their rituals indicate that their social life bears a lot of resemblance with the social behaviour of common langur.

Threats to Survival

1. Poaching for its hide and skin.
2. Habitat loss and habitat disturbance in many parts of its habitat.

Conservation Measures

Capped Langur is placed in Schedule–I of Wildlife (Protection) Act, 1972, thus ensuring a countrywide legal protection. Several protected areas have been declared in its distribution range to protect its habitat as well as the animal from poaching. In India, this animal is best seen at the Gibbon Wildlife Sanctuary and Kaziranga National Park in Assam. Though the local status of the Capped Langur is common, yet IUCN has declared it as Endangered.

HOOLOCK GIBBON

Order: Primate

Family: Hylobatidae

***Bunopithecus hoolock* (Harlan)**

Common Name

Holou bandor (Assamese), *Ulluck* (Hindi/Bengali), *Uluman* (Bengali), *Hulu makhra* (Bodo), *Heru* (Garo), *Hulu* (Khasi), *Yommu* (Manipuri), *Haluk* (Mizo), *Amepa* (Idu Mishmi), *Saka-huli*, *Chekkah* (Wancho), *Tooboung*, *Myouk umaigyau* (Arakanese).

Present Status

Wildlife (Protection) Act, 1972	Schedule–I
IUCN	Endangered
CITES	Appendix–I
Local Status	Uncommon

Distribution

Worldwide Distribution

The Hoolock Gibbon was formerly distributed widely across the eastern India, through Bangladesh to China and south to the Irawaddy River in Myanmar, northern

Thailand and northern Laos. Now the current population exists throughout the southern and eastern parts of Brahmaputra River in Assam (India) and Chittagong Hill tracts in Bangladesh, as well as in south Yunnan Provinces in China (northern Shan States) and Myanmar.

Distribution in India

In India, the Hoolock Gibbons are found in the forests of lowland areas in Assam, in the southern and eastern part of the Brahmaputra River and eastern part of the Dibang River; also recorded in Dibang Valley, Lohit, Tirap and Changlang districts of Arunachal Pradesh.

Habitat

Hoolock Gibbons are found in tropical evergreen rain forest, semi-evergreen forest, tropical mixed deciduous forest and subtropical broad-leafed hill forest from plains to 2000 m above the sea-level. It prefers the closed canopy or three-tiered forest vegetation with high, middle and low tier trees. Trees in the high tier provide space for sleeping, resting and sun-basking; whereas trees in the middle and low tiers provide food and paths for locomotion.

Distinctive Characters

Hoolock Gibbon is a small arboreal creature and the only ape found in India. It has the distinctive build of an ape; arms are much longer, almost double the length of its legs measured from hip to heel and body is without tail. It exhibits sexual dimorphism: the male is fully black with characteristic white eye-brows, and young females are also similar in appearance. However, adult females are faded to a golden or buff or yellowish-grey colour. A newly born Hoolock Gibbon is with yellow-tinted greyish-white hair, but turns dark within a couple of weeks.

The head and body length of an adult Hoolock Gibbon usually measures 46–63 cm. A female weighs about 6.0–6.6 kg and a male weighs about 6.1–7.9 kg.

Behavioural Biology

Hoolock Gibbon is arboreal in habit and almost entirely spends its life on treetops. It is diurnal in habit and during the hot hours of the day it takes rest in the lower and shadier branches of the trees with a unique posture by keeping its head burried between its legs. It moves either by a specialized, swing-arm type of locomotion by leaping or jumping between the trees or by bipedally walking on tree trunks or on the ground, when the distance is not reachable. While walking on the ground, it usually holds its long arms above the head, to maintain balance. They are good swimmers.

Gibbons, songs are the loudest of all calls in the northeastern forests and vocalized as "hookoo-hookoo-hookoo". With the daylight and warmth, hoolocks begin to howl; single group sings songs at a time, other groups wait for their turn.They remain quiet during the hottest hours of the day and again start howling in the evening.Each group is said to hunt within its own territory, where it follows the same trail through treetops day after day.

Feeding Behaviour

Hoolock Gibbon is frugivorous and majority of its diet comprises of fruits (mainly figs). They also eat leaves, flowers, buds and a small amount of insects, grubs and spiders. Occasionally they visit the cultivated lands to feed on them.

Reproductive Behaviour

Hoolock Gibbon generally mates early in the rainy season. Usually male choose a single mate. Gestation period is about 195–210 days. In the winter months (November to early February) female gives birth to a single young. The time between every birth is usually 2–3 years. The newborn infant always holds around its mother's belly tightly with the help of its legs and totally dependent on her milk upto six months of age. The mature newborn spends most of times playing with other group members and by feeding, always shares the night bed with its mother until another baby is born. Both the sexes attain sexual maturity at the age of 6–7 years.

Social Organization

Hoolock Gibbons live in small, monogamous family groups ranging from 2-6 individuals consisting of a mating pair and their offsprings. Social activities such as grooming, playing and sun basking are very common. The family groups maintain a definite territory ranging between 15–35 hectares; although the size varies with the number of family members. Usually they defend their territory by making loud territorial songs.

Threats to Survival

1. Habitat loss and fragmentation of habitat due to shifting of cultivated lands and deforestation for timber.
2. Hunted by local tribal people in Assam.
3. Gibbon's meat and bones are used in preparations of oriental medicines.

Conservation Measures

According to IUCN, Hoolock Gibbon is designated as Endangered, its local status is Uncommon and it is placed in the Schedule–I of Wildlife (Protection) Act, 1972, providing the animal a nationwide legal protection. Being in the Appendix–I of CITES, its use in international trade is being prevented.

Habitat destruction and fragmentation is the main cause of decline in population of Hoolock Gibbon in India. Therefore, planned afforestation programme should be undertaken to bridge the gaps and to make a continuous corridor for the movement of these gibbons from one place to another in search of food. More and more areas where these animals occur in good numbers should be declared as conservation areas.

TIBETAN ANTELOPE or CHIRU

Order: Artiodactyla

Family: Bovidae

***Pantholops hodgsonii* (Abel)**

Common Name

Chiru, Chuku, Tsus (%), *Chus* (&) (Tibetan)

Present Status

Wildlife (Protection) Act, 1972	Schedule–I
IUCN	Endangered
CITES	Appendix–I
Local Status	Uncommon

Distribution

Worldwide Distribution

Chiru is endemic to the Qinghai-Tibetan plateau and is found primarily in the Trans-Himalayan deserts of northwest Tibet in the remote Chang Tang area of China. Outside China, *Chirus* are only found in the Ladakh of Jammu and Kashmir in India.

Distribution in India

At present, in India *Chiru* occurs in only two small areas of Chang Chen Mo Valley of northern Ladakh, in Jammu and Kashmir. About 200 individuals (mostly males) migrate seasonally by crossing the Tibet border through Lanak La Pass.

Habitat

Chiru prefers grassy-flats for rolling and also Alpine steppe or similar semi-arid habitats at an altitude ranging from 3250 to 5500 m. Although it can readily ascend high rounded hills and penetrates mountains by crossing through passes.

Distinctive Characters

Tibetan Antelope has peculiarly swollen snout especially in males. Each nostril bears a large lateral chamber or sac, which may assist in high-altitude breathing. They also possess inguinal or groin glands, which are used for scent marking. Between the fore and hind hooves large scent glands are also present.

Its body is covered with dense wool and the colour varies with season. The winter coat is grey above with white underfur (known as 'shahtoosh' or the "king of the wools") and the summer coat is reddish in appearance. The whole face, mainly the upper side is dark brown or black and without any facial glands. Also there is dark brown stripe in front of both fore and hind legs. Males are with horns, but females are hornless.

Chiru stands 83–100 cm at the shoulder and horns measure between 60 to 65 cm. Females weigh about 26 kg; males are heavier than females and about 40 kg of weight.

Behavioural Biology

Movement pattern of the *Chiru* complex and is distinctly different between male and female. Males and females share same ground during winter, at the time of rut. They are usually seen in small groups of males or sometimes both males and females.

Chirus are known to dig bowl-shaped hollows in sandy and silty soil, which are roughly circular and measuring 110–120 cm in diameter and 15–30 cm in depth. They graze in the morning and in the evening and during mid-day, they take rest in the hollows made by them. Sight and sense of smell is keenly developed. The *Chiru* is an efficient runner with an average speed of 80 km/h.

Feeding Behaviour

The *Chiru* is both a grazer as well as browser. It feeds mainly on grasses and small vegetations. In summer months when the river plains are full of grasses they graze upon them and sometimes travel to high altitudes. During winter, they descend to lower altitudes and depend upon sprouting grasses.

Reproductive Behaviour

The Tibetan Antelopes generally mate in the winter months (November-December). Gestation period is about 7–8 months. In the second half of June and early July the females give birth to a single young. The females attain sexual maturity at the age of 1.5–2.5 years.

Young females remain with their mothers, but most of the males at 10 to 11 months of age leave their mothers and join mixed (adult and immature male) herds. In captivity, they can survive upto 8 years.

Social Organization

Depending upon the sex and season the herd size may change. Except female-offspring relationship, all other associations are unstable. Three types of herds are evident: all-male herds (consisting of immature and adult individuals); female herds (consisting of females with their offspring); and mixed herds (consisting of one or more animals of both sexes).

Threats to Survival

1. Poaching is the main threat to its survival. It is being slaughtered illegally for its wool. The underwool of *Chiru* is internationally known as 'shahtoosh' or 'king of wool' and is considered to be one of the finest animal fibres. Shahtoosh shawls and scarves are sold in the West for as much as US$10,000 each.
2. Habitat loss due to the expansion of domestic livestock herding, fencing of rangeland and economic development.
3. Horns of this antelope are used in traditional Chinese medicine.

Conservation Measures

According to IUCN, *Chiru* or Tibetan Antelope is designated as Endangered and its local status is Uncommon. This antelope is placed in the Schedule–I of Wildlife (Protection) Act, 1972, which provides highest legal protection to this species in our country. Presently several organizations have come forward for the protection of this species. Wildlife Trust of India, one of the leading non-governmental organizations, is working for this cause by habitat estimation, awareness generation and strict enforcement of Wildlife (Protection) Act, 1972. As weaving of the *'Shahtoosh shawl'* is exclusively done in the Jammu and Kashmir, the shatoosh weavers are also being persuaded not to weave these shawls. Alternetively, technologies have been provided to them which has enabled them to weave better quality shawls like *pashmina, shahmina* etc. To prevent any part of it from being used in wildlife trade, *Chiru* is included in the Appendix - I of CITES. Monitoring of its population in the wild, captive breeding and habitat preservation is essential to save this antelope.

NILGIRI TAHR

Order: Artiodactyla

Family: Bovidae

***Hemitragus hylocrius* (Ogilby)**

Common Name

Varai aadoo (Tamil); *Mulla aatu* (Malayalam); *Kard aardoo* (Kannad)

Present Status

Wildlife (Protection) Act, 1972	Schedule–I
IUCN	Endangered
CITES	No Special Status
Local Status	Locally common

Distribution

Worldwide Distribution

Nilgiri Tahr is an endemic species and is found nowhere in the world except India.

Distribution in India

This goat is endemic to southern parts of India. It is found in small pockets in Western Ghats, Nilgiri Hills of Tamil Nadu and Annamalai Range of Kerala upto an altitude of 1300-2600 m. They are best seen at Eravikulam National Park in Kerala.

Habitat

The preferred habitats of Nilgiri Tahrs are the montane grasslands and rocky crags; interspersed with shola forests at altitudes ranging from 1,200–2,200 m. They occasionally graze in the areas of grassy upland downs, the characteristic of South Indian hills.

Distinctive Characters

Nilgiri Tahr is a close relative of its Himalayan cousin–the Himalayan Tahr. They are slightly larger than the Himalayan Tahrs and stand 100–110 cm. at the shoulder. The males have a short, blue-black coat with a saddle shaped patch across the shoulders and back. Throat, abdomen and undersurfaces are pale and whitish in colour. However, the females and youngs are grayish brown to dark yellowish brown in colour. Males are much heavier than the females. The horns in both males and females are almost in contact at the base, rise parallel and then diverge and curve backward. These horns are closely set and deeply wrinkled.

Behavioural Biology

They are terrestrial animals and are diurnal in nature; always try to keep themselves above the forest. Their vision is quite sharp and they can run very fast once they perceive slightest of threat. They are very much wary in the wild. During the hot afternoon when the herd rests, one or more conspicuous females known as 'sentinel' stands guard. Considering the inaccessibility of their terrain, Nilgiri Tahrs are exceedingly watchful against any danger approaching from below and are least concerned of the dangers coming from the top. As a consequence, they are soft targets as prey for the leopards.

Feeding Behaviour

Nilgiri Tahr is strictly vegetarian in nature. Their preferred foods include various grasses, herbs, leaves and young shoots. They are grazers and forage in the early hours of the day as well as in the evening. During daytime they take refuge in the crags and rocks inside their habitat.

Reproductive Behaviour

Information regarding breeding behaviour of Nilgiri Tahr is scanty. Their breeding season is extended during a greater part of the year and females generally give birth to one young at a time usually at the commencement of the summer. However, sometimes two youngs are born at a time. The old males come out of the herd during hot summer months and are mostly found solitary.

Social Organization

The Nilgiri Tahrs are social animals and they always remain in groups, usually occur in herds of 10–15 individuals. Sometimes, more than one herd mix with each other, resulting about 100 individuals in a single herd. Females nurse and care for their offspring until they are self-sufficient.

Threats to Survival

1. Poaching is the main cause of their decline in numbers, as Nilgiri Tahrs are valuable source of protein, as well as income for local people.
2. Habitat loss due to agriculture and eucalyptus and wattle plantations.
3. Competition for grazing with domestic livestock.

Conservation Measures

Nilgiri Tahrs have been protected by Wildlife (Protection) Act in India since 1972. Several protected areas have been declared in its distribution range and are best sighted at the Eravikulam National Park in Kerala. This species breed well in captivity. Therefore, captive breeding and reintroduction can be a possible way of increasing their population size in the wild. Ecological studies are essential to form a basis of management plans since sustainable harvesting and/or licensed sport hunting of a restored population could be a valuable source of protein and income for local people in a safe and legal manner. In 1986, the estimated population size of the Nilgiri Tahrs was 2,000–2,200, relatively unchanged since 1978. Available evidences suggest that the three large populations have remained approximately stable in recent years. The largest known populations consist of nearly 550 animals each existing in the Eravikulam and Nilgiri Hills National Parks, comprising approximately 50 per cent of the remaining animals. The remaining populations are of less than 100 animals.

MARKHOR

Order: Artiodactyla

Family: Bovidae

***Capra falconeri* (Wagner)**

Common Name

Markhor (Punjabi/Kashmiri); *Rapoche* (♀), *Rawache* (♂) (Ladakhi)

Present Status

Wildlife (Protection) Act, 1972	Schedule–I
IUCN	Endangered
CITES	Appendix–II
Local Status	Rare

Distribution

Worldwide Distribution

Currently the distribution of Markhor runs from the mountains north of the Amur Darya River in Turkmenistan, east through Afghanistan, Pakistan and Northern India.

Distribution in India

In India, the distribution range of Markhor falls into the extreme northwestern part of Jammu and Kashmir.

Habitat

Markhor, live under varying conditions at altitudes ranging from 700 m during November to May and up to 4000 m in the summer. Different kinds of Markhor can be recognized depending upon the patterns of horns; also they live in different habitats. Markhors with most divergent horns live mostly in open forest areas; where as, Markhors with less divergent horns live in the dense pine and birch forests, in the Pir Panjal, Suleman and Kaj-i-nag ranges. Markhors live on the barren and bare slopes and are well adapted to intense cold in winter and extreme heat in summer. They generally do not cross the snow-line, as they do not possess underwool. In winter months they migrate to comparatively lower levels.

Distinctive Characters

Markhor is the largest mountain goat in the world. Height at shoulder is 80-100 cm. Females weigh between 30–40 kg and males between 80–110 kg. Markhors have long furs, a flowing beard and corkscrew horns. Body colour of males varies from rusty iron-grey in winter and reddish brown tinge in summer. Body colour of old males becomes more or less white. Young males do not possess prominent beard like adults. Females are usually darker than males and about half the size of a full-grown male and sometimes possess a scanty beard. Both the sexes have dark brown muzzles, brown upper legs. The belly and lower legs are creamy white in colour.

Behavioural Biology

They live in mixed herds, but in order to coexist, goats and sheeps acquire different habitats to overcome conflict, the goats occupy cliffs and their immediate vicinity and on the other hand, sheeps prefer the plateaus above cliffs and the gently sloping areas below them. Markhor forages 8–12 hours daily, and usually active throughout the day except for several hours during mid-day, when it rests and chews its cud. Like other goats Markhor is a good climber of trees.

Feeding Behaviour

Markhor is generally a grazer and browser. In the spring and summer, it mainly grazes on tussocks of grass. When these have dried up it browses on leaves and twigs, including the leaves of trees such as evergreen oak. The Markhor climbs trees in search of nutritious leaves. It can be seen standing on a branch of an oak tree 4–6 m above the ground, without hesitation.

Reproductive Behaviour

Mating generally occurs during winter and gestation period is about 135–170 days. Birth takes place from late April to early June. Females generally give birth to one or two fawns, rarely three. A young Markhor is weaned at 5–6 months and become mature at the age of 18–30 months. They can survive upto 13 years of age in the wild.

Social Organization

Although some adult males remain with the females throughout the year, but most males join the females only during the rut. Sometimes they can be seen in the group of 4–5 individuals.

Threats to Survival

1. Intensive hunting for trophies and meat.
2. Habitat loss and disturbance due to expanded human settlement and competition from domestic livestock.
3. Markhor horns are highly priced in traditional medicine. In China, 1 kg of horn may price up to US$1000.
4. The Markhor horns are one of the most desired of all hunting trophies, with a record horn length exceeding 1.5 m.
5. Prone to several diseases.

Conservation Measures

According to IUCN status, Markhor is designated as Endangered. Its local status is Rare and therefore it is placed in the Schedule–I of Wildlife (Protection) Act, 1972, which provide this species with a highest degree of nationwide legal protection. Hence, killing of this mountain goat may lead to punishment with penalty and/or imprisonment. After evaluating the threat of this species due to poaching and subsequent trade, it has been included in the Appendix–I of CITES, thereby preventing any of its body parts being used in trade. The habitat of Markhor falls under military control and it is difficult to implement Wildlife Protection Laws. However, presently the army personnel are being sensitized about the necessity for the protection of wildlife through several workshops and meetings by different organizations and are made aware about several provisions of the Wildlife (Protection) Act so as to indirectly involve them in protection of wildlife in these difficult terrains.

ASIATIC WILD BUFFALO

Order: Artiodactyla

Family: Bovidae

***Bubalus bubalis* (Linnaeus)**

Common Name

Arna (%), *Arni* (&) (Hindi), *Bonoria moh* (Assamese), *Jongli mosh* (Bengali), *Jungli mhais* (Marathi), *Menjek* (Adi).

Present Status

Wildlife (Protection) Act, 1972	Schedule–I
IUCN	Endangered
CITES	Appendix–II
Local Status	Locally common

Distribution

Worldwide Distribution

Asiatic Wild Buffalo originally ranged from eastern Nepal and India, east to Vietnam and south to Malaysia. Royal Manas National Park in Bhutan, Kosi Tappu Wildlife Reserve in Nepal and Huai Kha Khaeng Wildlife Sanctuary in Thailand inhabits the other sub-population of the Asiatic Wild Buffalo.

Distribution in India

In India, Asiatic Wild Buffalo are now mostly restricted to plains of Brahmaputra River in Assam of northeast India, in some parts of Orissa (Koraput District) and adjoining Bastar District of Chattisgarh of Central India.

Habitat

Asiatic Wild Buffaloes prefer habitats with low-lying alluvial grasslands and adjoining areas. They are very much dependent on the availability of water and tall grass jungles in the vicinity of swamps which provide them both food and shelter. In the riverine flats of Assam and Terai they lie in the pools of water and wallows themselves in mud. In the southern parts of their range, they live in the riparian forests and woodlands provided with nullahs.

Distinctive Characters

Asiatic Wild Buffalo is slaty black in appearance; the lower portion of their legs are dirty white. They are considered to be one of the fiercest animals with magnificent sweep of horns and sleeker, heavier and more robust look. The newborns are light coloured and almost yellow in appearance. The horn measures up to 197.6 cm and two types of variations in horn shapes can be seen in the wild buffalos: in one, the horns curve upwards in a semicircle and the tips are separated by small gaps; in others, the horns spread outwards almost horizontally from the head and curved slightly upwards and bent inwards near the tips. Both types may be found in the same herd. A large bull stands 170 cm at the shoulder and may reach even 200 cm and weighs about 800–1200 kg.

Behavioural Biology

During mid-day heat, they frequently wallow in the water of marsh or muddy pools, sometimes almost completely submerged except only its nostrils. Wallowing helps them to keep cool and also to remove skin parasites, biting flies and other pests. They generally avoid human being and where there are substantial human interference it becomes adapted for nocturnal mode of life. They often visit the cultivated lands. Asiatic Wild Buffaloes are described as the boldest and most savage among all the Indian mammals under family Bovidae. A bull may charge without any provocation and the females with their newborn calf are more desperate and dangerous. Sense of smell and hearing are well developed, but their sight is not very efficient.

Feeding Behaviour

Asiatic Wild Buffalo is mainly a grazer and feeds in the morning and evening, sometimes at night depending upon human disturbance. They remain in dense cover or wallows in water of marsh or muddy pools during mid-day. They prefer to eat grass and leafy aquatic vegetation of marsh.

Reproductive Behaviour

Their rutting season is at the end of the rains. Gestation period is about 300–340 days. The females usually give birth to one calf in the months of March-May. The birth interval is usually about 2 years. They can survive upto 25 years of age in the wild and upto 29 years in captivity. They become sexually mature at the age of 18 months. Asiatic Wild Buffalos, generally young and mature bulls that are driven from the herd during the rutting season, interbreed and frequently mate with domestic ones.

Social Organization

A herd of female Asiatic Wild Buffaloes with young is led by a dominant matriarch and is often accompanied by a single adult bull. Generally males are solitary in nature but sometimes bachelor males form their own herd having 10 individuals. They mix with females at the time of rutting.

Threats to Survival

1. The most important threat to Asiatic Wild Buffalo is interbreeding with feral and domestic buffaloes.
2. Habitat loss/degradation.
3. Hunting for meat and leather.
4. Diseases and parasites (transmitted by domestic livestock).
5. Competition for food and water between wild buffalo and domestic stock.

Conservation Measures

Although according to IUCN Asiatic Wild Buffalo is designated as Endangered, yet it is Locally Common and it is placed in the Schedule–I of Wildlife (Protection) Act, 1972, providing the animal a nationwide legal protection. Most of the areas of their concentration have been declared as conservation areas. Being in the Appendix–III of CITES, prevents any part of it from being used in international trade.

People living in and around their range are very much dependent on forest resources which lead to tremendous pressure on the grazing land. Thus, a development strategy involving the local people to be initiated so as they may utilize the forest resources but maintaining the quality of the forests. Fodder to be cultivated in all available waste lands around the forests so as to reduce the pressure on the grazing land within it. This will also reduce the chances of infection of the Asiatic Wild Buffalo from domestic cattle. However, several organizations (both government and non-government) have presently come forward to protect this species in its natural habitat.

GREATER ONE-HORNED RHINOCEROS

Order: Perissodactyla

Family: Rhinocerotidae

Rhinoceros unicornis **(Linnaeus)**

Common Name

Gainda (Hindi), *Gondar* (Bengali), *Gaur* (Assamese), *Genda* (Maratha)

Present Status

Wildlife (Protection) Act, 1972	Schedule–I
IUCN Status	Endangered
CITES	Appendix I
Local Status	Locally common

Distribution

Worldwide Distribution

Greater One-horned Rhinoceros is distributed in Pakistan, India, Nepal and Bangladesh.

Distribution in India

In India, distribution of One-horned Rhinoceros includes Terai area of north and northeastern India extending upto Chitwan area in Nepal with isolated patches in Assam and northern West Bengal.

Habitat

The Greater One-horned Rhinoceros inhabits dense jungles of tall elephant grass either on plains or in swampy areas near rivers. They also prefer to live in the dense riverine forests. However, due to habitat loss they have been forced into more cultivated land and even sometimes feed in cultivated fields and pastures.

Distinctive Characters

Greater One-horned Rhinoceros is a huge animal with a thick blackish skin folded to form characteristic folds or shields with scarce hairs. An adult male is about 300–380 cm long with a height of about 175–200 cm at shoulder and weighs 1800–2700 kg. It has a pointed, prehensile lip. There is one medially placed horn on the snout, which is composed of closely matted horny fiber and keratin. It is not connected with the skull bones. However, a slight enlargement of the nasal bone provides support to the horn. One medium sized horn measures about 37–40 cm (rarely 60 cm). The only hair visible in the body of One-horned Rhinoceros is at the ends of the ears and at the tip of the tail. Their vision is poor but the senses of hearing and smell are acute. Average lifespan of this animal is 30–35 years in the wild.

Behavioural Biology

Greater One-horned Rhinoceros remain more or less solitary. They usually seek to escape rather than attack an enemy. When wounded or when with calf, they occasionally charge. In such defense charges, contrary to the popular belief, they use their sharp pointed tusks in the lower jaw, not the horn. Most of the day they spent by resting, mostly wallowing in the mud. Rhinos often wallow and bathe in the muddy pools during the hot hours of the day; this helps them both for thermoregulation and avoiding flies.

They follow the same walking paths while foraging and also use the same spots to defecate forming well-defined toilets. Urination spots and rubbing sticks seem to serve the function of territory marking. Normally they confine their movements to a small area of about 0.75–5 sq km that act as their 'home range' and meet most of their requirements of food, water and shelter. Males wander further in search for their mates.

Feeding Behaviour

Greater One-horned Rhinoceros feeds on grasses, reeds, twigs and shoots. They generally feed during morning and evening. When two rhinos meet, ritualized behaviour, a series of displays and postures, involving curling of lips and baring the sharp tushes accompanied by snarls and grunts usually decides who is dominant and violence is avoided. However, in several occasions physical battle settles the dispute. These fights are noisy and sometimes lengthy affairs and can lead to serious injury and in rare instances the losers are mortally wounded.

Reproductive Behaviour

In the wild, February to April is the breeding season for Greater One-horned Rhinoceros. After a gestation period of about 16 months, a calf (exceptionally two) is born. At birth, the rhino calves are pink in colour and weighs about 60 kg. The mother and the calf stay together for three to four years. The female parent, meanwhile, mates again and get ready to produce another offspring.

Social Organization

Greater One-horned Rhinoceros is generally solitary except for females with young. Territories of males are not well-defined and sometimes overlap. Some loose aggregations between few individuals certainly occur at wallowing ground and foraging areas.

Threats to Survival

1. The horns of Greater One-horned Rhinoceros are used in traditional oriental medicines, especially as an aphrodisiac. The price of a processed horn may reach upto US$30,000 per kg. Therefore, killed by poachers.
2. Rhino skin, blood, urine and dung also have economic value.
3. Habitat destruction due agriculture and grazing by domestic livestocks.
4. Susceptible to diseases, like hoof and mouth disease, from domestic livestocks.
5. Large cats sometimes predate on young rhinos.

Conservation Measures

Total number of individuals of Greater One-horned Rhinoceros is estimated to be around 1700. *Rhinoceros unicornis* is severely threatened by hunting activities due to the huge economic value of the horn. This species is listed as Endangered by the IUCN. Being on the Appendix–I of CITES, prevent any part of this species being traded. In our country also this species is provided with highest degree of legal protection by enlisting this species under Schedule–I of the Wildlife (Protection) Act. Current projects are underway to reintroduce populations in areas where they have been extirpated. Efforts to control poaching and illegal wildlife trade will help in the recovery of the Indian rhino. One population in Nepal is protected with 700 armed troops and rangers, almost 2 guards per rhino. Aside from overhunting, the loss of alluvial plain habitat to agriculture has resulted in a reduction of suitable rhino habitat. In India, initiatives have successfully been taken to safeguard this species in its natural habitat and several protected areas (Kaziranga National Park–Assam, Gorumara National Park and Jaldapara Wildlife Sanctuary–West Bengal) have been declared. As a consequence of these conservation measures over the past few years, the number of rhino population have increased. Moreover, special force is working in these natural strongholds of Greater One-horned Rhinoceros under project "Operation Rhino" to safeguard them from the poachers.

ASIAN ELEPHANT

Order: Proboscidea

Family: Elephantidae

***Elephas maximus* (Linnaeus)**

Common Name

Hathi (Hindi); *Haati* (Bengali, Assamese); *Hasti, Gaja* (Sanskrit); *Aane* (Kannada); *Aana* (Malayam); *Yanai* (Tamil); *Hatti* (Marathi)

Present Status

Wildlife (Protection) Act, 1972	Schedule–I
IUCN	Endangered
CITES	Appendix–I
Local Status	Common

Distribution

Worldwide Distribution

Asian Elephant is distributed in India, Ceylon, Myanmar, Thailand, part of China, Malayasia and Indonesia.

Distribution in India

In India, Asian Elephant is found in two pockets, one is north Indian population continued till states of east and northeast India, whereas the south Indian population is distributed the south Indian states. In India, these animals are found in the states of Assam, Meghalaya, Manipur, Mizoram and Arunachal Pradesh in northeastern India; West Bengal and Orissa in eastern India; Jharkhand and few parts of Bihar and Chattisgarh in central India; Uttar Pradesh, Uttaranchal in northern India and Tamil Nadu, Kerala and Karnataka in the southern India.

Habitat

Asian Elephants prefer mixed deciduous and evergreen forests interspersed with scrub jungles and grasslands. They are more frequent in areas of tall forests with hilly and undulating grounds and also prefer areas with dense bamboo vegetation. However, they are found in steamy humid jungles, forest at higher altitude and colder climates too.

Distinctive Characters

Asian Elephants are the largest land mammals found in India. These animals usually have grey wrinkled skins and sometimes have light blotches over the body. Their body has only few long stiff hairs. However, a tuft of hair is present at the tip of the tail that is used for batting away insects. The forehead of Asian Elephant is tall and flat. Its long trunk (proboscis), that is a combination of nose and upper lip, has a single finger like projection at the tip. In contrast to its African counterparts, Asian Elephant has smaller ears; four nails in each hind foot instead of three and only the males bear tusks, which are actually the elongation of incisors of the upper jaw. The females have very small dental protrusion, extends only few inches outside their lip and are known as 'tushes'. Some males called 'makhnas' are tuskless too and can be distinguished from the females by the presence of penis bulging below their tail. The Asian Elephant has small eyes, rounded back and two-domed forehead. The adult males stand 245–275 cm at shoulder and weigh around 3000 kg.

Behavioural Biology

Asian Elephants are terrestrial animals and generally lead a diurnal mode of life. They migrate over a long distances in pursuit of food, water and in search of security. Average lifespan of Asian Elephant is 70 years in the wild. They traditionally use same pathway known as 'corridor' to migrate from one place to another. Once these corridors are destroyed or blocked by human habitations then they enter human settlement, which often leads to human-elephant conflict. In pursuit of food they also raid crop fields close to their original habitat or nearby their corridor. Most frequently, they are attracted to the human habitation by the smell of country liquor. Their eyesight is not that keen which is compensated by their acute sense of smell and hearing.

Asian Elephant, being a social animal, communicate between the members of a herd by means of various sounds. A loud trumpeting noise is used to gather a herd. A hollow resonant sound made by tapping the trunk on a hard surface with the tip turned upward while snorting appears to be alarm signal. They have a large combination of sounds *viz.* growls, roars, grunts, trumpeting and snorts for specific type of communications, like warnings, greetings, distress and signaling. The herd generally keeps to the denser forests during hot and dry seasons. However, during rains they come out into open stretches and enter the cultivations. Elephants sleep during the hot hours of the day and again retire to sleep after midnight. Asian Elephants rest standing or stretched on its side. They flap ears to cool the blood inside the vessel close to the surface of the ear. They love to bathe and shower themselves with water and afterward with dusts to repel insects.

Feeding Behaviour

Asian Elephants are strictly herbivorous in nature. Their food consist of various kinds of grasses and leaves, shoots and leaves of wild bamboos, all species of crops, food grains and barks of specific kinds of trees. A full grown adult consumes around 270-320 kg of green fodder and drinks 30 gallons of water daily. As a matter of fact, the elephants have a larger home range as compared to other terrestrial mammals and practice seasonal migration. They feed early in the morning and evening and come out to raid crop or to feed in the open forests after darkness sets in. During the dry seasons, the larger herds break into smaller groups to explore different habitats and again reunite once the condition is favourable. The tuskers feed keeping a distance from the main herd. The herd generally follows a regular and synchronized routine of drinking and feeding at specific places. However, succulent crops like sugarcane, banana etc. and distilleries of country liquor allure these large animals and they frequently raid those places.

Reproductive Behaviour

The exact breeding season of Asian Elephant is uncertain, but breeding season is believed to be during summer till the commencement of rainy season. Gestation period lasts for 18–22 months. After completion of the gestation period generally single young is born, mostly during late autumn. However, giving birth to the twins is not unknown. Once, a calf is born, the other female members of the herd provide good care for both the mother and her baby. They assist the female parent to take care of her calf as well as they themselves act as guardians to the newborn calf. The calves weigh about 90–100 kg at birth.

Females reach sexual maturity between 9–15 years of age while males reach sexual maturity at 15 years. Male elephants (rarely females) show peculiar periodical signs of excitement on attaining sexual maturity, mostly during the cold season, which is known as 'musth'. An elephant in musth usually shows some sort of erratic behaviour and generally seeks for a mate.

Social Organization

Asian Elephants are social animals and have a wide complex of community laws, rules and regulations, a marked discipline and many well-established customs. They live in a matriarchal society. Each herd consists of 15–30 individuals led by an old female known as 'matriarch'. Herds are believed to be composed of single families and consist of chiefly females, immature elephants and one or few old tuskers. However, stray females and young males may migrate from one herd to another.

Males have home ranges of about 15 sq km and herds of females of about 30 sq km (larger in the dry season).

Threats to Survival

1. Poachers kill male elephants for their tusks, leading to disruption in male-female sex ratio.
2. Habitat loss due to agriculture extentions and deforestation.
3. Death or injury caused by railway accidents.
4. Loss of elephant corridors due to construction of industries, railway tracks and highways.
5. Ever increasing Human-Elephant conflict as wild elephants often enter the human settlements in search of food.
6. Diseases

Conservation Measures

Asian Elephant being placed under Schedule–I of the Wildlife (Protection) Act, 1972, is legally protected throughout the country and killing or harming Asian Elephant as well as the destruction of its habitat is prohibited. To protect this animal from the poachers, it is placed under Appendix–I of the CITES. This means that the trade in any part of an Asian Elephant is illegal and are subject to strict punishment. Asian Elephants have a long history of being hunted by people, originally for food, later for domestic stock and ivory. Poaching for ivory continues to devastate wild populations. They also suffer from habitat loss caused by agriculture and deforestation. Centuries ago they disappeared from southwestern Asia and most of China. Currently there are only an estimated 28,000 to 42,000 wild Asian Elephants remaining. Asian Elephants are kept as domestic animals and can be successfully bred in captivity to a limited extent. In the year 1991, the Ministry of Environment and Forests, Government of India had launched "Project Elephant" to save the Asian Elephants existing in India. At that time such an initiative was the need of the hour as this species was then critically mired with several problems–like poaching of the tuskers for their tusks which was smuggled to feed into the ivory market of the far east and a subsequent skewed sex ratio of male and female elephants, habitat destruction, human-elephant conflict, electrocutions, accidents etc. As a consequence, the number of Asian Elephants had declined alarmingly. Though several problems still exist and a constant vigil is always necessary to safeguard this species, however, it can be said that this project has helped considerably to revive the population of the Asian Elephants and has pulled them back from the verge of extinction.

SLENDER LORIS or VANGU

Order: Primate

Family: Loridae

Loris tardigradus malabricus **(Linnaeus)**

Common Name

Chinge koollie (Kodava), *Kaadu pappa, Adavi manushya, Mala manushya* (Kannada), *Thevangu* (Tamil, Malayalam), *Devanga pilli* (Telugu).

Present Status

Wildlife (Protection) Act, 1972	Schedule–I
IUCN	Endangered
CITES	Appendix–II
Local Status	Uncommon

Distribution

Worldwide Distribution

Slender Loris is found only in the tropical rain forests of India and Sri Lanka.

Distribution in India

In India, Slender Loris is mainly concentrated in the southeastern part of the Western Ghats. Two races of this species are reported to occur in India.

Habitat

Slender Loris lives in dry and wet forest, of lowland and highland (200–950 m). They have a wide range of habitat–rainforest, deciduous, shrub, cool mountain forest, swamps etc. It generally prefers thick thorny vegetations, which they use to escape from predators and ensure large assortment of insects.

Distinctive Characters

Slender Loris is about the size of a chipmunk, measuring between 15–25 cm in total body length and with a small vestigial tail. Weight is about 225–340 gm. The arms and legs are long and pencil-thinned. Second digit of both the hands and feet are characteristically very short. Head is large, rounded with two large, closely set, saucer-like dark brown or black eyes. Eyes flank with a long nose which ends in a heart-shaped knob. Eyes are surrounded by a dark brown circle of fur, while the bridge of the nose is white. Lower jaw is small and narrower. Ears are small, rounded. The fur is less dense, but soft and woolly. Coat colour varies from dark-grey to red-brown on its back, much paler underside with dirty white coloration.

Behavioural Biology

Slender Loris is arboreal and spends most of the time of its life on trees. Their movement is slow and precise and prefer top branches, but also can move quickly. They generally climb trees by grasping branches strongly with their opposable thumbs and toes.

In the wild, they are solitary or may live with a mate and an infant. Usually hunt alone or in groups sharing a common food supply and sleep with others in a hollow tree or sitting up on the angle of branches. In captivity, may tolerate each other; lead a social life by playing, wrestling and grooming each other and females may care the babies of other females. Very aggressive when kept together, engage themselves in constant quarrelling and fighting, sometimes resulting to death.

They also engage themselves in rubbing urine over hands, feet and face, probably to soothe and defend against the sting of toxic insects. Their forward looking eyes are adapted to night vision and have an owl like appearance. They have unique habit of swaying from side to side and make slow chattering noises and utter a low growl when disturbed. Slender Loris is able to tolerate high environmental temperature largely due to their ability to increase evaporative cooling.

Feeding Behaviour

Slender Loris sleeps by day, remains hidden among foliage or in a hole or crevice and starts foraging at dusk. It is mostly insectivorous and hunts insects, lizards, small birds, tree frogs, occassionally eggs and consumes everything of its prey including feathers, scales, bones and exoskeleton. They have a fondness for the berries of lantana bushes that grow profusely in scrub jungles. They can stretch and twist their long arms and legs through the branches without alerting their prey. Slender Loris eats a lot of noxious and bad smelling insects, also like toxic beetles and roaches.

Reproductive Behaviour

Slender Loris mates twice a year, generally in the months of April-May and October-November. Gestation period is about 166–169 days. In the months of May-June the females give birth to single, occasionally two individuals. Newborns have thin fur and eyes do not open for several weeks. Females become reproductively mature at 10 months and male at 18 months of age. They can survive upto 12-15 years.

Social Organization

Newborns are quite helpless; grasp their mother around the waist with fore and hind legs. After few weeks, mother 'parks' the infant on a branch during foraging at night. At first, babies move around carefully and by two months of age manoeuver around quite well. Mature lorises may visit them at night to play and eat with them.

Threats to Survival

1. It was believed that all parts of Slender Loris have some medical and magical power, which had led to illegal killing of this species.
2. Destruction and alteration of habitat.
3. Being used as an experimental animal.
4. Restricted distribution.
5. Previously not much attention has been paid to the plight of the species.

Conservation Measures

According to IUCN, Slender Loris or Vangu is designated as Endangered, its local status is Uncommon and it is placed in the Schedule–I of Wildlife (Protection) Act, 1972 and is incorporated in the Appendix–II of CITES. Since it is a very good trade commodity, the experts suggest that this species should be included in Appendix–I of CITES to check any kind of exploitation by trade (both international as well as trade within the country). Moreover, census of this species is necessary to evaluate its present population status. However, census of Slender Loris is indeed difficult.

RED PANDA

Order: Carnivora

Family: Ailuridae

***Ailurus fulgens* (Cuvier)**

Common Name

Wah, Ye, Nigalva, Ponva (Nepalese); *Oakdonga, Wakdonga, Woker* (Bhotia); *Sankam* (Lepcha).

Present Status

Wildlife (Protection) Act, 1972	Schedule–I
IUCN	Endangered
CITES	Appendix–I
Local Status	Rare

Distribution

Worldwide Distribution

Red Panda is found in the temperate forests with bamboo understorey between 1500 m to 4000 m in Himalayas, high mountains of northern Myanmar, western Sichuan and Yunnan provinces of China. This stretch of distribution includes Nepal, India, Bhutan, northern Myanmar and China (Yonzon, 1989; Pradhan *et al.*, 2001).

Distribution in India

In India, range of Red Panda distribution encompases three states–West Bengal, Sikkim and Arunachal Pradesh. Recent report of ocurance of Red Panda is also received from Meghalaya (Chaudhury, 1997). In the state of West Bengal, Red Panda is present in the Singalila National Park and Neora Valley area in the hilly district of Darjeeling. Red Panda in Sikkim has been reported from Kunchendzonga National Park (northwest Sikkim), Fambong Lho Wildlife Sanctuary and Kyangnoisia Alpine Sanctuary (east Sikkim), Shingba Rhododendron Sanctuary (north Sikkim) and Barsey Rhododendron Sanctuary (west Sikkim). In Arunachal Pradesh, presence of Red Panda has been reported from the Eagle Nest Wildlife Sanctuary (Mukherjee, 1994; Kakati, 1996). Other protected areas where Red Pandas are present, include Mouling National Park, Namdapha National Park, Mehao Wildlife Sanctuary, Pakhui Wildlife Sanctuary, Kamlung Wildlife Sanctuary, Dibang Wildlife Sanctuary, Tawang Wildlife Sanctuary, Lado Wildlife Sanctuary and Palin Wildlife Sanctuary (Rodgers and Panwar, 1988).

Habitat

Red Panda lives in the temperate forest of the Himalayas above the 1525 m or so on. In general, nocturnal in habit, the animal spends its day sleeping on trees. During rests, it is curled up in the topmost branches, with its bushy tail wrapped over its head, or it lies along a branch with its head tucked away under its chest between its forelegs. In the evening, it descends to the ground and hunt for food and climb back to its roost in the morning.

Distinctive Characters

Head is round; rostrum is shortened and the ears are large, erect and pointed. The body of Red Panda is covered with long, coarse guard hairs and the undercoat is soft, dense and wooly. The fur on the upper sides of its body is reddish-brown, while ventrally it is glossy black. The furry tail is marked with about 12 alternating red and buff rings and is not prehensile. The face is predominantly white with reddish-brown 'tear' marks under its eyes. Its legs are black and the soles of its feet are covered with dense white hair. There is no sexual dimorphism in color and size between males and females. Their front legs are angled inward, leading to its waddling walk and its feet are plantigrade.

Head and body length–510 mm to 635 mm; shoulder height–273 mm to 283 mm and tail length–280 mm to 485 mm. Their weight varies in between 3.70 to 6.20 kg.

Behavioural Biology

Red Panda is most active at dusk, dawn and during the night. The movement on the ground is done by a slow, cross-extension gait and a faster bounding or trotting. They are arboreal, sleeping in nests usually built in evergreen forests. They descend trees headfirst and display their flexibility as they move from branch to branch. The tail is used for balance when the Red Panda is on the tree and while on the ground the panda carries it straight and horizontally. They engaged in several leisure behaviours after awakening and eating. It licks its whole body and limbs, washes its face with forepaw and hindpaw and stretches or rubs its back and abdomen against a stationary object such as a tree or a rock.

Feeding Behaviour

In the wild, Red Panda searches for roots, succulent grasses, leaves and fallen fruits. Eggs, insects and grubs may also be part of the diet–depending on individual taste. They feed on fresh bamboo leaves only at the base of the stalk and do not eat the stalk itself.

In captivity, they take bananas, apples, sweat bread, honey, sugar, milk etc. Generally honey, sugar and eggs are mixed with milk. Every day, each Red panda also provided with 2 kg bamboo (*Arundinaria maling* or so called 'maling bamboo') leaves.

Reproductive Behaviour

The male home ranged generally overlap and may even expand in the mating season. Individuals scent mark their territories and home ranges with urine and secretion from anal glands, present on the soles of their feet. They use these 'scent spot' as regular latrine sites and communicate information that helps to maintain social spacing and undoubtedly convey information about sex, age and reproductive condition of the depositor. Red Pandas use subtle body language, including head bobs and tail arching, including a threatening 'huff-quack' and alluring 'twitter' and warning 'shistle' to communicate at close range.

Generally winter months (December–February) is the mating season. There is a delayed implantation period, as in bears and embryogenesis is about 50 days. Females become noticeably heavy and lethargic around six weeks before parturition. Several days before parturition, the female begins to carry nest materials (stick, grass, leaves) to a suitable nest site. In the wild, a nest may be a hollow tree or a rock crevice. Gestation period is approximately 131 days. The youngs (usually 2–4 in number) are born in the spring months (May–July). Newly born Red Panda is blind but fully fur covered. Body and tail lengths are 20 cm and 5 cm respectively. The young attain adult size at around 12 months and become sexually mature at around 18 months. They can survive upto 14 years in captivity, but probably a lot less in the wild.

Social Organization

Red Pandas typically live alone, but sometimes form pairs or small family groups. The young and mother share a close relationship until the young becomes aggressive at the onset of the next breeding season.

Threats to Survival

1. Hunting, trapping and trading. Red Pandas skins are found quite commonly in local markets in China. There appears to be some illegal trade of Red Pandas between China and Taiwan. In China, a Red Panda skin worn by the bridegroom in the wedding ceremonies of one of the local indigenous people.
2. Some animals are hunted as food to a limited extent by some tribal people and some are persecuted for crop-raiding and chicken-killing.

3. Habitat loss and fragmentation of habitat (mainly by local people for fuel and fodder requirements).
4. Cannibalism of the young by parent.
5. Red Pandas suffer from diseases like respiratory problems, pneumonia, edema, congestion, toxemia, septicemia, lipidosis and fatty degeneration. In recent years, it is observed that one of the most important diseases of Red Panda is canine distemper.
6. The trade of live Red Panda to zoos was formerly very prevalent. However, legislation has probably limited this practice in most recent years.

Conservation Measures

According to IUCN status, Red Panda is designated as Endangered and its local status is Rare. It is placed in the Schedule–I of Wildlife (Protection) Act, 1972 which provide the animal a nationwide legal protection. Several protected areas have been declared within its distribution range. To prevent international trade of any of its parts, it is included in the Appendix - I of CITES. Red Panda has been declared as the *"State Animal"* of Sikkim and was the mascot of the International Tea Festival in Darjeeling. Regarding the conservation of Red Panda, sufficient protected areas exist for reintroduction to be successful. The population is so low and fragmented that this may have deleterious genetic effects through inbreeding.

Current population size and status of the Red Panda in Singhalila and Neora Valley National Parks is an indicator of their global status. WWF India has initiated conservation measures in the distribution ranges of this unique species. *Ex-situ* conservation has been initiated through development of a specific captive breeding facility within the existing area inside the Padmaja Naidu Himalayan Zoological Park, Darjeeling for the purpose of captive breeding as well as to initiate an extensive research program. Initiation of *in-situ* and *ex-situ* research programs for successful reintroduction of individuals deemed suitable on the basis of a biological assessment of their capabilities to survive in the wild. Monitoring the whole Red Panda population with a particular emphasis on population dynamics, the actual biological impact of such a release, exploring the possibility of release in other areas and subsequent actions can conserve Red Pandas in their natural habitat as well as increase their number through successful conservation breeding programmes and reintroduction of those pandas in the wild.

ASIATIC WILD DOG or DHOLE

Order: Carnivora

Family: Canidae

***Cuon alpinus* (Pallas)**

There are 10 subspecies of the *Dhole* ranging in color and size. Two of the subspecies are listed as Endangered by the IUCN (East Asian *Dhole* and the West Indian *Dhole*). Two other subspecies are on the verge of extinction (*C.a. primaerus*, and the *C.a. laniger*). However, only three subspecies of *Dhole* live in India in the Trans-Himalayan, Himalayan and Peninsular region.

Common Name

Dhole, Janglee kutta, Ban kutta (Hindi); *Kolsun, Kolsara* (Marathi); *Kutra, Kol kutta* (Gujarati); *Kadu nai* (Kannada); *Rezu kutta* (Telugu); *Chen nai* (Malayalam/Tamil); *Ram kutta, Jonglee kukur* (Bengali); *Rang kukur* (Assamese); *Baliya kukura* (Oriya); *Huithon* (Manipuri); *Ramkun* (Kashmiri); *Farra* (Ladakhi); *Sidda ki* (Tibetan)

Present Status

Wildlife (Protection) Act, 1972	Schedule–II
IUCN	Endangered
CITES	Appendix–I
Local Status	Locally common

Distribution

Worldwide Distribution

Wild Dogs are widely distributed in central and eastern Asia from Altai mountain and southward through the forests of India, Bangladesh and Malayan countries.

Distribution in India

In India, Wild Dogs are found in peninsular, central, northeastern and southern states as well as in the Himalayan regions from Ladakh to Sikkim. They are distributed in the states of Jammu and Kashmir, Himachal Pradesh, Uttaranchal, Uttar Pradesh, Bihar, Jharkhand, Chhattisgarh, Andhra Pradesh, Orissa, West Bengal, Sikkim, Assam, Arunachal Pradesh, Meghalaya, Mizoram, Manipur, Tripura, Madhya Pradesh, Kerala, Karnataka and Tamil Nadu.

Habitat

Wild Dogs prefer open forests interspersed with grassy lands or meadows. They are found in varied type of habitats starting from the dry deciduous forests to the moist evergreen forests. They generally prefer shaded places with available water inside the forest. However, in Ladakh and Tibetan region they are found mostly in the open lands in absence of forest in the uplands. They are never found in the open plains and deserts.

Distinctive Characters

Wild Dog has some similarity with the domestic dog but with a slender body and reddish brown coat. However, the coat colour varies from sandy brown to rust red and the individuals towards southern India have a deeper coat colour. They have shorter legs, more bushy tail with a black tip and the ears are more rounded at the tip as compared to the domestic dog. Its muzzle is shorter and thicker from both wolf and domestic dog. Their dental formula is different from that of the wolf, jackals and domestic dogs and lower jaw contains six molar teeth in spite of seven of the others. Therefore, *Dholes* are considered to be one of the primitive dogs. Females of the wild dogs bear 12–14 tits on the ventral side of their body. Their pups are shooty brown in colour at birth and within three months take the hue in their coat.

An adult male weighs about 20 kg and stands about 43–55 cm at shoulder. Total body length of Wild Dog is about 90 cm. However, the female dogs are lighter and slightly shorter.

Behavioural Biology

Wild Dogs are carnivorous in nature. They prefer to live in places where there are abundance of food and shade and are very fond of water. They use water to drink as well as to spend time in lying down in those waters to keep themselves cool especially during summer. They have also been spotted sitting in shallow pools of water regardless of the temperature. Just as domestic dogs, *Dholes* wag their tails and there is no evidence of aggressiveness among pack members (except for the cubs, who like to play fight) and there is almost never any bullying.

Feeding Behaviour

Pack of *Dholes* feast on mammals ranging from rodents to deer, preferably on wild pigs, hares, wild goats, sheeps and occasionally monkeys. Larger mammals are attacked from the rear, while smaller ones are caught by any part of the bodies and a swift blow to the head kills the smaller mammals. Wild Dogs eat very fast and an adult can eat up to 4 kg of meat in one hour and begin to feed on it before it is dead. Two to three individuals can kill a 50 kg deer.

Reproductive Behaviour

Each pack contains a dominant monogamous pair and subordinate pack members help to care for the youngs, of the dominant pair. The gestation period is about 60–62 days. The mother usually gives birth to eight pups at a time usually at the end of winter and the first spring months (November–March). Female having up to 16 tits, suggests their ability to take care of large number of pups. Dens are generally constructed near stream beds or among rocks. After a female has given birth, a few other adults take part in feeding the mother as well as the pups.

Social Organization

Wild Dogs live in packs ranging from 5–12 individuals and also interact with other members outside of their own group, but the original pack rarely exceeds twenty. They prefer cooperative group hunting and group care of young.

Threats to Survival

1. Habitat loss and degradation of habitat due to agriculture and infrastructure development.
2. Decline in the prey species or food source increases dependency on domestic livestock causing man-animal conflict.
3. Persecution (mainly poisoning) of *Dholes* living outside or on the edge of the protected areas, by local peoples.
4. Competitions for prey species with other large animals like tiger, leopard etc.
5. Diseases and pathogens (canine distemper, parvo virus and rabbies) transmitted by feral and/or domestic dogs.

Conservation Measures

In India, *Dholes* are protected under Schedule–II of the Wildlife (Protection) Act, 1972 (permission is required to kill any individual unless in self-defense or if an individual is a man killer). The creation of Tiger Reserves in India has provided some sort of protection to this animal. However, experts suggest that the poisoning of this animal may affect the remaining *Dhole* populations. The Wild Dogs mostly occur in the protected areas present throughout its distribution range. No conservation measure has yet been taken up, especially to protect this species. However, in India, *Project Tiger* could potentially maintain their prey base in areas where Tigers and *Dholes* coexist. This species is listed under Appendix–II of CITES, which prevents international trade of its body parts.

Colour Plates

Pygmy Hog *Sus salvanius* (Hodgson) (Page No. 17)

Asiatic Lion *Panthera leo persica* (Meyer) (Page No. 20)

Golden Langur *Trachypithecus geei* (Khajuria) (Page No. 32)

Capped Langur *Trachypithecus pileatus* (Blyth) (Page No. 35)

Tibetan Antelope or Chiru *Pantholops hodgsonii* (Abel) (Page No. 10)

Nilgiri Tahr *Hemitragus hylocrius* (Ogilby) (Page No. 43)

Asiatic Wild Buffalo *Bubalus bubalis* (Linnaeus) (Page No. 49)

Greater One-horned Rhinoceros *Rhinoceros unicornis* (Linnaeus) (Page No. 52)

Asian Elephant *Elephas maximus* (Linnaeus) (Page No. 55)

Red Panda *Ailurus fulgens* (Cuvier) (Page No. 62)

Asiatic Wild Dog or Dhole *Cuon alpinus* (Pallas) (Page No. 66)

Tiger *Panthera tigris tigris* (Linnaeus) (Page No. 69)

Snow Leopard *Uncia uncia* Schreber (Page No. 72)

Hispid Hare *Caprolagus hispidus* (Pearson) (Page No. 75)

Brow-antlered Deer or Sangai *Cervus eldii eldii* (M'Clelland) (Page No. 83)

Swamp Deer or Barasingha *Cervus duvaucelii* (G. Cuvier) (Page No. 87)

Indian Bison or Gaur *Bos gaurus* (H. Smith) (Page No. 94)

Sloth Bear *Melursus ursinus* (Shaw) (Page No. 103)

Clouded Leopard *Neofelis nebulosa* (Griffith) (Page No. 107)

Fishing Cat *Prionailurus viverrinus* (Bennett) (Page No. 113)

Blue Sheep or Bharal *Pseudois nayaur* (Hodgson) (Page No. 124)

Himalayan Musk Deer *Moschus chrysogaster* (Hodgson) (Page No. 126)

Leopard *Panthera pardus* (Linnaeus) (Page No. 132)

TIGER

Order: Carnivora

Family: Felidae

Panthera tigris tigris
(Linnaeus)

Common Name

Bagh, Sher (Hindi); *Wagh* (Marathi); *Poolee* (Tamil and Telugu); *Kaduwa* Malayalam); *Hoolee* (Kannar); *Char* (Burmese); *Bagh* (Bengali)

Present Status

Wildlife (Protection) Act, 1972	Schedule–I
IUCN	Endangered
CITES	Appendix–I
Local Status	Uncommon

Distribution

Worldwide Distribution

Six different races of Tigers have been distinguished over the wide area of its ange. The Indian race however, is found in Nepal, Bhutan, Bangladesh, Myanmar nd India.

Distribution in India

The animal is found throughout the country from Himalayas to Cape Comorin, xcept in the deserts of Rajasthan, in Punjab, Kutch and in the Sind. The range of ndian Tiger extends upto Myanmar.

Habitat

Tigers are found in the humid evergreen forests, in dry open forests, in the grassy swamps of the Terai and even in the mangrove forests like Sunderbans. In Sunderbans, the tiger leads an almost amphibious life in a terrain with mangrove trees, mud and water. Three components are essential for a tiger–healthy prey base, ample vegetation cover and shade to sleep in and drinking water. In India, the Tiger has left its tracks in the winter snows of the Himalayas at an altitude of 3050 m.

Distinctive Characters

An adult Indian Tiger measures about 300 cm in length and about 180–230 kg in weight. The graceful built and a majestic look of the tiger is well known. The rich reddish yellow to orange rufous coat marked with black stripes all over the body and the black ringed tail are characteristic features of this animal. Colour of the ventral surface is pale and whitish. The ears are black, each with a prominent round white spot on the outer side of the pinna. Tigers have prominent whiskers. The forelimbs consist of 5 digits and the hind limb consists of 4 digits with retractile claws.

The sexual dimorphism is very distinct in Tigers. The body size and the whiskers of the males are much bigger than the females. Presence of scrotal sacs in the males is another distinguishing character. During breeding season, conspicuous mammary gland is evident in the females. The mammary gland is found along the ventro-lateral side of the body from the axilla to the groin.

Behavioural Biology

Tigers are territorial animals and are predatory in nature. They form small family units, especially when the mother is raising her cubs. However, the adult males prefer to spend most of the time alone. Tigers are diurnal. Dawn and dusks are the time for grooming, when it spends long periods licking its paws, chest and back. On a hot day, they may even stroll to a stream or a water hole for a refreshing drink. Tigers are good swimmers and take to water readily. Though it is not arboreal in nature, but can climb trees as and when necessary.

The female parent provides maximum parental care. Association of male and female appears to end when the cubs are born, but there may be some companionship for a varying period after that. Territorial marking is present.

Feeding Behaviour

Tigers are strictly carnivorous in nature. It predates on deer, gaur, nilgai, antelope, wild boar, bear, porcupine etc. It has also been reported to kill elephant calves, leopards and sometimes even other tigers. Driven by hunger it will feed almost anything, fowl fish, reptiles or carrion. Many, in absence of game animals or from opportunity, take to cattle killing.

Reproductive Behaviour

Tigers are polyestrous animals and these animals are found to breed throughout the year. The estrous cycle occurs at 24 days interval. A receptive female shows different signs like restlessness, frequent micturition, unusual posture with legs directed upwards, occasional rolling on the ground and snores loudly. The gestation period is about 105 days. Generally two to three, but sometimes, as many as six cubs are born at a time and the cubs remain with their mother until about two years old. It is not known whether the tigers are strictly monogamous in nature.

Social Organization

Tigers are usually considered to be solitary. However, there are reports that although they hunt individually, a group of females within an area are mutually tolerant, meet frequently and even share their kill. The females share their area with a single male, to which they do not show hostility. On the contrary, the adult males are intolerant to each other and only one male is usually associated with each group of females.

Threats to Survival

The population of tiger is presently declining due to several natural and anthropogenic factors.

1. Destruction of the habitats of these animals is taking place due to illegal logging and indiscriminate felling of trees. This has resulted into shrinkage of its cover and reduced prey species.
2. Poaching of the animals for their hide and skin, nails and other body parts.
3. Several parasitic diseases.
4. Natural disasters like floods, super cyclones, forest fires etc.
5. Infighting between the adult tigers for protecting territory and for mate selection.

Conservation Measures

Tiger is protected by law and is included in Schedule–I of the Wildlife (Protection) Act, 1972, and under the Appendix–I of CITES. In 1974, a nationwide programme for the conservation of tigers was launched and subsequently 19 tiger reserves have been established throughout India. The countrywide ban on tiger hunting since 1972, setting up of tiger reserves in 1974 onwards, inclusion of tiger under Appendix–I of CITES has considerably reduced the killing of tigers and trade of its body parts. Stringent laws and their successful implementation have improved condition for our national animal. Moreover, improved and scientific management of the protected areas and tiger reserves and intense patrolling have made a significant difference to the tiger population of India.

SNOW LEOPARD

Order: Carnivora

Family: Felidae

***Uncia uncia* (Schreber)**

Common Name

Barfani Cheetah (Urdu), *Bharal He* (Pahari), *Palang-I-Barfi* (Berfy), *Shan* (Ladakhi), *Burhel haye* (Bhotia), *Sheen-e-suh* (Kashmiri), *Yuodi simyo* (Adi), *Thurwagh* (Kunawar), *Ikar*, *Zig*, *Sachak* (Tibetan Bhotia)

Present Status

Wildlife (Protection) Act, 1972	Schedule–I
IUCN	Endangered
CITES	Appendix–I
Local Status	Rare

Distribution

Worldwide Distribution

Snow Leopards are found in Afghanistan, Bhutan, India, China (Sichuan, Gansu, Inner Mongolia and Qinghai Provinces), Kazakhistan (Altai Mountains, Tian Shan Mountains, along the border between Kazakhistan and China), Kyrgyzstan, Mongolia (Altai Mountains, Hangai Mountains, and, farther west, in the Hanhohiy Uul and Harkhyra Uul ranges), Nepal (Himalayan chain along the Tibetan border), Pakistan (near the snow line in northern Pakistan), Russia (Sayan Mountains in southern Siberia), Tajikistan (Pamir-Altai range) and Uzbekistan (along the western end of the Tian Shan mountains).

The core areas of Snow Leopard habitat are present around the periphery of the Tibetan Plateau and Taklamakan desert in the Himalaya, Karakoram, Hindu Kush, Pamir, Kun Lun, Tian Shan, and Altai mountain ranges.

Distribution in India

In India, Snow Leopard is known to occur across the Himalayan range, including the states of Jammu and Kashmir, Himachal Pradesh, Uttar Pradesh, Sikkim and Arunachal Pradesh.

Habitat

Snow Leopards typically inhabit rugged terrain such as steep slopes with bluffs, ridges broken by outcrops and valleys interrupted by rocks and cliffs, with arid and semi-arid shrubland, grassland or alpine steppe vegetation above the tree-line at an altitude of 3000–4500 m above the sea-level. Snow Leopards generally avoid dense forest.

In summer months, it occasionally goes above 5500 m in the Himalayan range. But, at the onset of winter, like other animals of hilly areas, Snow Leopard migrates to low levels of 600–1500 m into the oak, fir and rhododendron forests.

Distinctive Characters

Snow Leopard is built to live in snow-covered areas at temperature upto –40°C. It has long, thick smoky grey fur with dark-grey rosettes and black spots on its limbs, which allows it to camouflage superbly. The wooly underfur is pure white. The tail is characteristically very long and thick. It has large, well-cushioned paws in comparison to its body, a strong chest and short fore limbs that enable it to leap around the cliff side. New borns are darker than the adults. An enlarged nasal cavity warms the air that it breathes and helps them to survive in extreme cold climate.

The female weighs 35–40 kg and the males are slightly heavier, weighs about 45–55 kg (sometimes up to 75 kg) and total head to body length is 100–130 cm.

Behavioural Biology

Snow Leopard is either crepuscular or nocturnal in habit. Generally take rest during daytime and hunt at night. It is an excellent rock climber and prefers travelling along linear pathways such as major ridgelines, gullies and the base or crest of broken cliffs.

Feeding Behaviour

Snow Leopards prey on wild pigs and gorals to Himalayan tahrs, markhors, takins, musk deers and argalis. However, their favourite prey species are blue sheep and ibex. In addition, marmots, hares and pikas are important among small mammals and sometimes they kill large birds too. In addition, all forms of livestocks represent significant prey items in some areas. Generally in the summer months, when the upland plateau is open for grazing, they get the opportunities to prey upon domestic goats, sheep or ponies from the herd. The cubs eat their first solid food when they are about two months old and a month later begins to follow their mother when she goes for hunting. They hunt with their mother at least through their first winter. Snow

Leopards are in general solitary and hunt alone, but at times a pair may travel together, especially during the rutting season.

Reproductive Behaviour

Mating usually takes place between late-January and mid-March. Gestation period is about 93–110 days. In the month of June or July the females give birth to 2 to 3 cubs. The youngs become sexually mature at 2–3 years of age. They can survive up to 21 years in captivity.

Social Organization

A female may be accompanied by 1–3 cubs until the youngs become one year or older. Home range varies from 12–39 sq km, even exceed upto 400 sq km, where there is scarcity of food. Male and female home range may overlap. Snow Leopards mark their territory by scraping the ground with their hind paws, scent-marking rocks and depositing other signs.

Threats to Survival

1. Snow Leopards are hunted for fur and trophies.
2. Killed by farmers because the farmers consider this species as a livestock predator.
3. Lack of its natural prey species as a consequence of large scale pika and marmot poisoning programs conducted on the Tibetan Plateau. This leads to the increased dependency of Snow Leopard on domestic livestock as prey species.
4. Increased use of bones of Snow Leopards in oriental medicine with the decline in availability of tiger bones.

Conservation Measures

According to IUCN status, Snow Leopard is designated as Endangered, its local status is Rare and it is placed in the Schedule–I of Wildlife (Protection) Act, 1972 providing the animal a nationwide legal protection. It has been included in the Appendix–I of CITES thus prevented from being used in international trade.

In India, the Padmaja Naidu Himalayan Zoological Park in Darjeeling started work on captive breeding project of this threatened mammal in the year 1983. On 21st March 1986, a pair of unrelated Snow Leopards were brought to Darjeeling from Zurich Zoo. Special attention was given to these species and the project Snow Leopard reached success.

However, field research and status survey of Snow Leopard is necessary to assess the present population status and distribution of this species. Snow Leopard, its prey species and habitat need to be protected. Control of over grazing-stocks in conservation areas should be prohibited. This in one hand will reduce the habitat degradation and on the other it will minimize the Human-Snow Leopard conflict that results from the killing of the domesticated livestocks by this species. There have been management proposals to provide villagers throughout Ladakh with the necessary construction material to protect their livestock-pens from the entry of Snow Leopards.

HISPID HARE

Order: Lagomorpha

Family: Leporidae

***Caprolagus hispidus* (Pearson)**

Common Name

Khargorkata, Khagorikota pohu (Assamese)

Present Status

Wildlife (Protection) Act, 1972	Schedule–I
IUCN	Endangered
CITES	Appendix–I
Local Status	Rare

Distribution

Worldwide Distribution

Hispid Hares are found in the patches of the Terai grasslands along the edge of the Himalayan foothills in India, south to Dacca in Bangladesh and the Terai region of southwest Nepal.

Distribution in India

In India, Hispid Hares have been recorded from Assam, northern parts of West Bengal (Duars), northwest Bihar, Madhya Pradesh and Uttar Pradesh.

Habitat

Hispid Hares live in Terai grasslands and forests of Himalayan foothills. They prefer to live in dense tall grasses commonly known as "elephant grasses" or thatches which generally grow upto 3 m during the monsoon season. Occationally, they move to foothills or cultivated fields when these grasslands adjacent to forests are set to fire at the beginning of the year or become waterlogged during monsoon.

Distinctive Characters

Hispid Hares are slow moving creatures with its characteristic rounded droppings. It is also called 'bristly rabbit'. Presence of brown dorsal hairs predominantly mixed with black hairs gives it a dark-brown appearance. Its rufous chest appears darker than whitish abdomen. Tail is much shorter, dorsally brown and ventrally paler in appearance. Ears are short and rounded and hindlegs are not much larger than the forelegs. The Hispid Hare weighs about 2–3 kg and total body length is 38–50 cm.

Behavioural Biology

Hispid Hares do not construct burrows, rather take shelter in surface vegetation or burrows made by other animals. It is a slow-moving creature. Presence of its pellets near the thatch cutting reveals its presence.

Feeding Behaviour

Hispid Hares generally feed on barks, shoots and roots of grasses, including thatch species and occasionally on crops.

Reproductive Behaviour

Very little is known about the breeding behaviour of Hispid Hare. Probably birth takes place from December to February as newborns are caught from January to March. Number of offspring varies from two to five.

Social Organization

It is not a gregarious animal, but sometimes seen in pairs of male and female.

Threats to Survival

1. Habitat loss due to human settlement, cultivation, forestry, grazing and the burning of thatch.
2. Killed for food and to protect crops.
3. Predation by dogs.
4. Changes in riverine vegetation due to human induced seasonal flooding.

Conservation Measures

According to IUCN, Hispid Hare is designated as Endangered, while its local status is Rare. Considering its present status, it is placed in the Schedule–I of Wildlife (Protection) Act, 1972 thus giving them appropriate legal protection. Most of the areas of their concentration have been declared as conservation areas like Manas

Biosphere Reserve (Assam), Jaldapara Wildlife Sanctuary (West Bengal), Balmiki Reserve (Bihar) and Dudwa National Park (Uttar Pradesh). It has been listed under the Appendix–I of CITES, which protect this animal to be used in international trade.

Instead of continuous burning of the thatches in their habitat during dry season, rotational burning of tall-grass habitat would provide suitable cover, food and protection to this species. Effective fire control and long-term management of habitat are needed in various conservation areas of their occurrence. Efforts to maintain Hispid Hares in captivity have been unsuccessful in the past. However, a long-term study on the behaviour and ecology is needed to formulate the future conservation strategies.

GANGETIC DOLPHIN

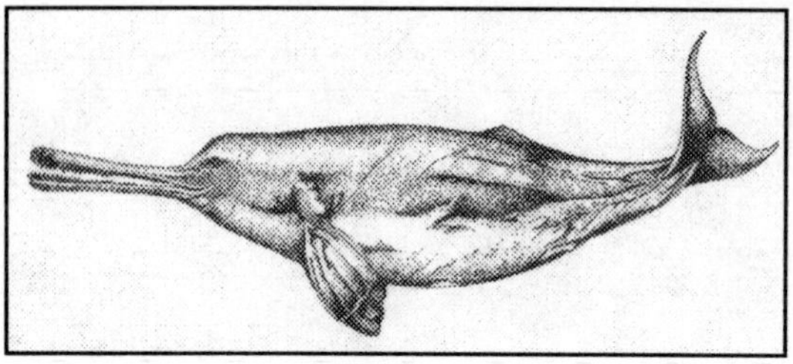

Order: Cetacea

Family: Platanistidae

***Platanista gangetica* (Roxburgh)**

Common Name

Sus, Susu (Hindi); *Susuk* (Bengali); *Hiho, Huh seho* (Assamese); *Sunsar, Bhoolan* (Sindhi), *Sinsumar* (Sanskrit)

Present Status

Wildlife (Protection) Act, 1972	Schedule–I
IUCN	Endangered
CITES	Appendix–I
Local Status	Uncommon

Distribution

Worldwide Distribution

Gangetic Dolphin is found in India, Nepal, Bhutan and Bangladesh in the Ganges, Brahmaputra, Meghna, Karnaphuli and Hooghly River systems.

Distribution in India

In India, Gangetic Dolphins are distributed in river Ganges, Brahmaputra and their larger tributaries upto the bases of the hills. These animals are best seen at Kaziranga National Park (Assam) and Vikramshila Wildlife Sanctuary (Bihar) within their distribution range. These true freshwater Cetaceans are also found in the tidal limits. However, they do not enter the sea.

Habitat

This species is the only true Cetacean found in India. They are aquatic in nature and lives in the muddy water of rivers.

Distinctive Characters

The colour of Gangetic Dolphin varies from lead to black and the ventral surface is lighter in colour. Body is fusiform and measures 1.7–2.5 m in total length. The tail fluke is on average 46 cm in width. It weighs between 70 and 85 kgs. Females are larger than male. Gangetic Dolphin has a characteristic prolonged snout forming a long narrow beak, bearing a row of sharp interlocking teeth. Both jaws contain teeth varying from 27–32 in numbers designed to trap prey. The rudimentary dorsal fin is ridge-like and the ends of the pectoral fins are squared instead of tapered. The neck is visibly constricted and the blowhole is a longitudinal slit. The eyes and optic nerves of this species are degenerated. The eyes lack lenses and are, therefore, incapable of forming images on the retina. However, it functions in light-detection. It is believed that the lack of a true visual apparatus in the river dolphin is related to its habitat; as the water in which it lives is so muddied that vision in essentially useless.

Behavioural Biology

Gangetic Dolphins are non-gregarious in nature and are found in small groups in certain parts of the rivers. They are very active and continuously make vocal sounds. They swim few inches above the river-bed. During summer, the migratory behaviour is prominent while during rainy season they descend to tidal waters and sometimes get trapped in the fishing nets.

Feeding Behaviour

Gangetic Dolphins browse the river-bed and feed on living crustaceans and catfishes. They also feed on shrimps and other smaller fishes.

Reproductive Behaviour

Very little is known about the breeding behaviour of this animal. Generally one or two young are born at a time. Gestation period is considered to be eight to nine months. Though Gangetic Dolphins can give birth to the youngs throughout the year, but most births occur between October and March. A significant birth peak takes place in December and January, at the beginning of the dry season. Generally they reach sexual maturity in ten years and they are reported to be sexually active even at the age of twenty-six.

Social Organization

The youngs are weaned and remain solitary before they are one year old.

Threats to Survival

1. Habitat destruction mainly through pollution of the rivers in their distribution areas, especially the pollution of the river Ganges affects this species very much.
2. Construction of large dams within their distribution areas.

3. Poaching of this species. Fishing nets and harpoons are used to capture these animals for their meat and fat. Oil extracted from fat is used for burning lamps and several other purposes.

Conservation Measures

The animal is listed as CITES Appendix–I, thereby legally preventing any part of this species being used in wildlife trade. This animal is hunted both for its meat and oil, which is used to fuel lamps. Other sources of threat include fishing nets, in which the river dolphin often becomes tangled when it migrates to tidal waters in the monsoon and dams which interfere in to its local migration and thus separate potentially breeding populations from one another. This aquatic mammal is categorised as Endangered under IUCN and is provided with the highest degree of legal protection throughout Indian territory as being placed in the Schedule–I of the Wildlife (Protection) Act, 1972. Research activities need to be promoted and status surveys should be initiated to assess the present population of the Gangetic Dolphin. Few non-government organizations have also come forward to prevent the killing of this species for their meat and fat. An alternative for the dolphin fat have also been identified which in turn will reduce the threat on these animals.

VULNERABLE

BROW-ANTLERED DEER or SANGAI

Order: Artiodactyla

Family: Cervidae

Cervus eldii eldii
(M'Clelland)

Common Name

Sangai, Thamin (Manipur), *Dancing Deer* (English)

Present Status

Wildlife (Protection) Act, 1972	Schedule–I
IUCN Status	Vulnerable
CITES	Appendix–I
Local Status	Rare

Distribution

Worldwide Distribution

The subspecies of Brow-antlered Deer found in India is *Cervus eldii eldii* and are found nowhere in the world except a pocket population in India. However, other subspecies like *Cervus eldii thamin* were found previously in Myanmar and the Malay Peninsula, and *Cervus eldii siamensis* in Thailand, Annam, and Hainan Island. The subspecies *Cervus eldii thamin* is now restricted to Myanmar. *Cervus eldii siamensis* is found throughout Hainan Island.

Distribution in India

This deer is endemic to India. In India, the Brow-antlered Deer is found in the wild only in Keibul Lamjao National Park, Manipur.

Habitat

Forests on the sandy plains, which are flooded seasonally and usually dominated by *Dipterocarpus tuberculatus* is supposed to be the main habitat for *Cervus eldii eldii*. They usually prefer open scrub jungles and are found to graze on the flat or undulating terrains between rivers and hill ranges. They are mainly found on or adjacent to the *Phumdis* of the Loktak lake inside the Keibul Lamjao National Park.

Distinctive Characters

An adult deer is nearly 120 cm high at the shoulder and weighing about 100–150 kg. It has distinct long hairs on its neck. The coat is coarse and sparse. The stags are dark brown or nearly black and the hinds are lighter. They had developed slightly sprayed–out hooves and their pasterns are hairless and horny so that they can walk with them on reeds and grasses and not sink through the "*phumdi*". The youngs are spotted. Their speed and sharp sight are their main defensive features. The colour of male is dark brown in winter and fawn in summer, whereas the female is light fawn in colour and the young is spotted. *Sangai* males have very unique and characteristic antlers, which they attain in the second year and reach its prime at the age of seven years. The antlers at the base form an almost erect pedicle, thereby diverging from each other. The profile of the outline of the horn is almost circular and from the tip of the brow-line upto the antlers, form a continuous curve.

Behavioural Biology

They are reported to be seen mostly in the early morning and late evening. They sometimes dance round and round with heads up and heads down. *Cervus eldii eldii* is mainly nocturnal and crepuscular and are reported to have both daily and seasonal migrations. These movements are largely influenced by breeding seasons and on the availability of food and water in various seasons.

Feeding Behaviour

Sangai comes out for feeding in the morning and evening from the thick-forested area. These animals are herbivorous in nature. *Cervus eldii eldii* is a species known to graze and browse opportunistically on wild fruits. It is reported that they also occasionally raids cultivated crops from the fields adjacent to their habitat in the fringes of the forest. They feed mainly on the grasses sprouting on "*phumdis*", leaves and fallen fruits. Their favourite food is the Ishing Kombong grass (*Saccharum latifolium*). There is no conflict among the deer population during the consumption of food. A few commonly eaten crops are rice, lentils, maize, peas and rape.

Reproductive Behaviour

Rutting season is between March and April. The stags shed their antlers during late June. Brow-antlered Deers breed only once a year and are not territorial in nature.

The male gets extremely restless at the onset of breeding season and the restlessness reaches such a degree that in the wild it can get into fight with anyone willing to compete with him for his chosen partner. This aggression can sometimes lead to fatal wounds. Females become reproductively matured at the age of two years and may reproduce till the age of ten years. During late winter or early spring, the females exhibit a prolonged period of ovarian activity of 225 to 342 days and undergo 10 to 17 estrous cycles. The gestation period lasts for 239–256 days and one fawn is born usually in October. The youngs are weaned at about 5 months of age. Polygamy or interspecific breeding behaviour is not distinct and no unique parental care is recorded.

Social Organization

During most of the year, the males tend to lead a solitary life, except during the rutting season in the spring. Females, on the other hand, tend to remain in close association with their fawns and other female-fawn pairs. Large groups consisting of two to twenty animals are often formed. Males join these groups of females with the onset of the breeding season. During this time they are reported to have a male to female ratio of 1:1.59, and a doe to fawn ration of 1:0.54. The home ranges reported to vary from 3.8 to 14.71 square kilometres.

Threats to Survival

1. Loss of habitat due to siltation, burning of grass, encroachment of human settlements, interference due to cattle grazing, damming, fishing, etc.
2. Illegal wildlife trade of their skin and antlers. Moreover, these animals were previously hunted as game animals and are used as a food source. They were prized as a game animal because of their antlers and hides.
3. Diseases such as tuberculosis, hepatic and enteric disorders, worms in the stomach and vitamin deficiencies.
4. Intra-specific fight during breeding season.
5. The captive population tends to remain small due to limited resources. Such small populations are vulnerable to both demographic and genetic problems. Inbreeding leads to the loss of genetic diversity of the animal affecting its vitality, vigor and survival of the newborn as well as the fertility of the individual animals.
6. Earlier, they have been used for "traditional" medicinal products and are poached for this purpose.
7. In addition, *Sangai* have become a major zoo animal, especially since their populations are decreasing in the wild.

Conservation Measures

Presently this animal is categorised as Vulnerable by the IUCN. Very limited number of individuals are presently distributed in the wild. Realizing the threats of extinction, these animals are provided with the highest degree of legal protection. This species is placed under Schedule–I under the Wildlife (Protection) Act, 1972 which means that killing and harming this species is subject to stringent punishment in the form of imprisonment or fine or both. The major habitat of *Sangai* has been notified as Keibul Lamjao National Park and the Loktak lake has been declared as a Ramsar site, a wetland of international significance. The species has also been listed under Appendix–I of CITES which prevents any part of it being traded. The subspecies, *C. eldii eldii* found in India has become so rare that its survival will eventually rely on the practice of gene exchange of the wild and captive organisms by means of assisted reproduction. This type of assisted breeding is being used in Thailand and Myanmar on the other subspecies as well.

SWAMP DEER or BARASINGHA

Order: Artiodactyla

Family: Cervidae

***Cervus duvaucelii* (G.Cuvier)**

Common Name

Barasingha, Maha (Hindi), *Dal horina, Bhelengi pohu* (Assamese), *Baradali horin* (Bengali), *Goinjak* (%), *Gaoni* (&), *Salsamar, Nerwari* (Central India), *Gonda, Gonr, Ghos* (Nepal Terai)

Present Status

Wildlife (Protection) Act, 1972	Schedule–I
IUCN	Vulnerable
CITES	Appendix–I
Local status	Locally common

Distribution

Worldwide Distribution

Swamp Deer is found in several localities in the Terai of southern Nepal and in India.

Distribution in India

In India, this species is currently found in Gangetic plains of Sunderbans (West Bengal), Assam, Madhya Pradesh, Terai and Uttar Pradesh.

Three subspecies of Swamp Deer have been reported till date–(i) Wetland Barasingha or *Cervus duvaucelii duvaucelii* found in Terai, Uttar Pradesh, Assam and Sunderbans; (ii) Upland Barasingha or *Cervus duvaucelii branderi,* only a single population in hard and open ground of Madhya Pradesh and (iii) *Cervus duvaucelii ranjitsinhi,* currently a single population is found in Assam and northeast India.

Habitat

In Terai, the Swamp Deer lives on marshland (swamps) and rarely go out of water, sometimes they wallow in muds. In Madhya Pradesh, they forage on grasslands close to forest zone. In Assam, they live in high ground in the proximity of water.

Distinctive Characters

This is a large-sized deer with average body weight of 170–180 kg and having a shoulder height of 115-135 cm. Body covered with wooly coat and coat colour varies depending upon season. In winter, the adult stags have dark brown coat and with manes. The summer coat of stags and hinds (females) is pale brown, sometimes with spots but not always distinguishable. The young deers are with spots. Male deers are provided with very distinct twelve-tined antlers that give this deer the name *Barasingha.* Although there are many variations present in the formation of antlers, but two distinct types with many intermediary patterns are distinguishable. The usual number of points is 10–14, but there may be as many as 20 points.

Behavioural Biology

They are active during the day or at night. They feed soon after daylight, again in the late afternoon and take rest during the daytime. They drink at least twice daily during the hot summer months, travelling to a water hole early in the morning and in the evening. The eyesight and hearing are moderately developed, but the sense of smell is acute. It is recorded that in captivity they can survive up to 23 years of age.

Feeding Behaviour

Swamp Deers feed mainly on grasses, but the population dwelling in and around the marshlands and swamps occasionally feed on aquatic and wetland plants.

Reproductive Behaviour

Mating takes place throughout the year, generally between September to April. Gestation period is about 240–250 days. In the months of August–November, the female gives birth to single individual. The time-span between two successive births is one year. The females become reproductively mature at the age of two years. During the peak of the rut this species is known to form breeding herds consisting of a number of adult males, females and youngs.

Social Organization

This species is highly gregarious in nature. In Terai, a swamp may contain thousands of individuals. In central India, the majority of the *Barasinghass* are found in mixed herds in a ratio of female to male 2:1 for first eight months of the year. For the rest of the year, the herds are smaller in size and many animals become solitary. Each herd may contain up to 30–50 individuals. Males generally establish a dominance hierarchy and the highest-ranking male taking priority to meet any estrous female.

Threats to Survival

1. Habitat loss and habitat modification due to wetland reclamation, grass and timber cutting, illegal gathering of fuel wood.
2. Poaching.
3. Diseases introduced by cattles.

Conservation Measures

Though it is Locally Common, however, IUCN has categorized Swamp Deer as Vulnerable considering its global population status and present threats. It is also placed in the Schedule–I of Wildlife (Protection) Act, 1972, providing the animal a nationwide legal protection. Most of the areas of their concentration have been declared as conservation areas. Being in the Appendix–I of CITES, any part of it is prohibited from being used in international trade. Reallocation of this species into new areas has also been suggested by the experts but an attempt to introduce the deer in Bandhavgarh National Park failed in the past.

URIAL or SHAPU

Order: Artiodactyla

Family: Bovidae

***Ovis orientalis* (Gmelin)**

This species has ten subspecies throughout the world, out of which *Ovis orientalis vignei* Blythe, 1841 is present in India and is known as Ladakh Urial.

Common Name

Urial (Punjabi); *Shapo (%)*, *Shamo* (&) (Ladakhi)

Present Status

Wildlife (Protection) Act, 1972	Schedule–I
IUCN	Vulnerable
CITES	Appendix–I
Local Status	Uncommon

Distribution

Worldwide Distribution

Urials are widely distributed in Asia minor. They are found from southwestern Kazakhstan through Turkmenistan, Uzbekistan, Tajikistan, Afghanistan, Pakistan and into the Kashmir region of India. They range eastward into Iran and some are found in Oman, although that population is thought to have been introduced. Urial or Shapu is found in the mountain areas of Russia, Pakistan, India and central Asia including Ladakh eastward to Tibet and southward and westward to Punjab, Sind, Baluchistan and south Persia.

Distribution in India

In India, these animals are distributed in the areas of Ladakh at Indus valley, Karakoram, Gilgit and Astor. It is also found at Skadu in the Pakistan-occupied Kashmir.

Habitat

Urials prefer to live in the grasslands of the alpine zones above the tree line. They are found in the steep grassy terrains upto an elevation of 6,000 m. They rarely move to the rocky areas of the mountains. Though it avoids the steep slopes and high rocky mountain cliffs, however, when needed can climb up those areas with remarkable ease. Their habitat tends to be moderately to very arid. They may also be found in agricultural fields and sometimes enter partly wooded areas (Valdez, 1982).

Distinctive Characters

The adult males of Urial have a reddish-brown coat with a black and white saddle patch and a black or grizzled throat ruff growing from either side of the chin, meet below and extends down the throat. With the onset of the summer, much of the ruff is shed. In older rams, the upper part of the throat ruff turns grey or white. The Urial has three races such as Afghan race, Punjab race and Ladakh race. The throat ruff is best developed in the Punjab race. In built, Urial is smaller than all other species of wild sheep. The average weight of an adult Urial lies between 35–90 kg and their height at shoulder varies from 70–90 cm. They have a pair of well developed strongly wrinkled horns that measure about 50–75 cm. However, a wide range of variation, exist in the orientation and architecture of their horns between different subspecies and a single herd within the same area as well. The face bib, under parts and the lower part of the legs are white. Females of the Urials or ewes do not show any saddle patch. The females have a lighter hue of coat colour and the youngs are smaller and greyish in colour. The horns of the females are shorter and the lateral stripes are present up to a black spot under its foreleg. The average lifespan of Urial is between 8–12 years (Valdez, 1982).

Behavioural Biology

These sheep are mainly diurnal and spend most of their day in foraging. They are terrestrial animals of the high altitude areas. They move throughout a range, but do not maintain territories (Valdez, 1982). Dominant males act as a stabilizing force in sheep society by preventing younger rams from harassing females. Young males are more aggressive and bullying towards ewes than the older males. Aggressive encounters between similar-sized individuals usually include head twists and front kicks. Urial sheeps do not rise on to back legs before clashing (Valdez, 1982). As they live in the grasslands and other open terrains, they remain very much wary and alert.

Details regarding communication in this species are lacking. However, it is known that males have aggressive physical encounters by which they establish and communicate dominance relationships. Tactile communication seems likely. Females communicate their estrous status to adult males via chemical cues in their urine. Also, mothers and infant recognize one another based on scent, so olfactory communication plays an important role in this species. It is likely that there is also some amount of acoustic communication, although this is reportedly not common (Valdez, 1982; Nowak, 1999).

Feeding Behaviour

Urials are herbivorous in nature. They feed on the grasses and young leaves of the plants present in the grounds where they graze. Unspecified plants, presumably grasses and shrubs compose major portion of their diets. However, they are also reported to feed on several grains.

Reproductive Behaviour

The breeding season of Urial varies in different subspecies. In summer, the females and youngs live together in small herds. During this time the adult males live apart separately. While a ram is in rut, he visits several herds in search of a grown up ewe in heat. It is only during the rutting season when the adult males reunite the herds with the females. In Punjab, the rutting season is between September and October; in Ladakh and Astor, the rutting season is further late. Once the rutting season is over, the entire herd breaks into smaller parties of 5–6 individuals, comprising of one ram and 3–4 females. Urial males are polygynous, but males do not maintain a harem. Males approach females slowly in a stretched posture. The female reacts by squatting and urinating. The males then smell the female's urine to understand if the female is in estrous. The dominant male claims a female in estrus and after copulation, this dominant male guards the female from other males until she is no longer in estrous. Once the female is no longer receptive, the male will leave in search of another female in estrus (Valdez, 1982). Ewes become sexually mature at 1.5 years of age and may bear their first young at two years of age. Period of estrous lasts for 1–2 days. Copulation is speedy, lasting a mere 2–3 seconds. The gestation period of Urial is believed to be 5–6 months and the youngs are borne during summer. Young pregnant females upto the age of 3 years, on each occassion give birth to one lamb. However, older ewes may give birth to 2–3 lambs.

Social Organization

Urials are gregarious and form herds of related individuals. Herds usually comprised of females, lambs and juveniles. Each of these social units generally consists of 10–30 individuals. Adult rams form separate all-male groups. Separation of herds eliminates competition for foraging and reduces female harassment. Herds have a social structure in which dominance is based on body size. Dominance relationships are especially evident in ram herds, where dominance is largely based on horn size—the larger the horns, the higher the dominance rank (Valdez, 1982; Nowak, 1999).

Threats to Survival

1. Habitat Loss/Degradation–Infrastructure development and human settlement and consequently extraction of wood, expansion of agriculture in wild sheep habitat and other human habitat modifications (Nowak, 1999).

2. Harvesting (hunting/gathering)–Poaching for skin, horns, flesh and wool.
3. Natural disasters like droughts, temperature extremes, avalanches, landslides etc.
4. Changes in native species dynamics including competitors, predators, pathogens, parasites etc.
5. The current population of *O. vignei* is estimated at less than 1,500 individuals occurring in two fragmented populations. Loss of habitat and hunting pressures are thought to be contributing to a continued decline in the population.
6. It is considered especially vulnerable because it inhabits the low, open country where people commonly graze their livestock (Nowak, 1999). This makes these animals especially susceptible to competition from domestic livestock for food resources.
7. Intrinsic factors–Low densities, restricted range.

Conservation Measures

Ladakh Urial is placed in the Schedule–I of Wildlife (Protection) Act, 1972, thus legally protected in India. Several protected areas have been declared with in its distribution range. Being in the Appendix–I of CITES, they are prohibited from being used in international trade. Experts suggest that their present population need to be strictly conserved and the habitats in which these animals are found need to be protected from any further degradation. Involving local people in the process of Urial conservation may reduce the conflict.

INDIAN BISON or GAUR

Order: Artiodactyla

Family: Bovidae

***Bos gaurus* (H. Smith)**

Common Name

Gaur (Hindi); *Kattee, Kattee pothook, Paothu* (Malayalam); *Kattu erumai* (Tamil); *Gariya, Gawa* (Marathi); *Kartee* (Kannada), *Gayal* (Oriya)

Present Status

Wildlife (Protection) Act, 1972	Schedule–I
IUCN	Vulnerable
CITES	Appendix–I
Local Status	Common

Distribution

Worldwide Distribution

Gaur or Indian Bison is found in India, Nepal eastward to Myanmar and Malay Peninsula.

Distribution in India

In India, this animal is found in the southern part of Maharashtra, southward to the Western Ghats. It is also found in the central and southeastern Peninsula, Orissa, West Bengal and the northeast Indian states of Arunachal Pradesh, Meghalaya, Manipur, Mizoram, Tripura and Nagaland.

Habitat

Gaurs inhabit mixed deciduous, scrub and evergreen hill forests and grasslands. Gaurs essentially live in the hilly terrains. However, at certain seasons, they descend downward. In the Himalayan region, they stay in the foothills and are reported to climb at a height of 2000 m or more in the peninsular India.

Distinctive Characters

Characteristic features of Gaur are a massive body, deep chest, large head, sturdy limbs and muscular ridge upon its shoulders. The coat of an adult bull is hairless and glossy deep black with a characteristic ashy forehead and yellowish and white coloured feet. However, the newborns are golden-yellow and gradually changes its colour to light-brown to red-brown and finally to coffee-brown. Its tail is comparatively short with a small black tassel. Both sexes have well developed pointed horns. An adult bull weighs 800–1200 kg and stands 165–195 cm at shoulder.

Behavioural Biology

Gaur is very shy, calm and timid as compared to its size. However, a wounded Gaur as well as solitary bulls may charge without provocation. These animals generally avoid human habitation, do not enter cultivated fields or feed on agricultural crops. They are terrestrial animals and are found active both during daytime and night. Their eyesight and sense of hearing is poor. They have an acute sense of smell, which along with their massive size and horns are the measures for their defense. If taken by surprise, the entire herds run in an indefinite manner and sometimes even stampede their own calves.

Feeding Behaviour

The chief food of these animals comprise of grasses, young bamboo shoots, leaves and bark of trees. It forages from late evening to early morning in the forest areas and open meadows in between. In cool or clouded weather, they also graze in the afternoon. However, during hot hours of the day, they take shelter and stay in the shaded places inside the forests avoiding the scorching sun. They also have the habit of visiting 'salt licks' present in their distribution range. The Asian Elephants and Gaurs are frequently found grazing together out of which Gaur derive benefits. They prefer feeding high bamboo shoots and such foliages are out of their reach unless pulled down by the elephants while feeding.

Reproductive Behaviour

During breeding season, bulls roam widely through the forest, stopping at intervals and making a clear, resonant, 1–3 seconds long mating calls. Call is repeated at a descending scale and more frequent calls are heard at dawn and dusk. At the peak of the breeding season, rutting calls are heard throughout the night. These roaming males search females in heat and when successful defend the female from other males until they mate. These rutting males do not establish any territory and neither protect the herd exclusively. Rutting season of Gaur is March-May and the newborns are seen from November–March. Just before parturition, the pregnant female moves away from herd to give birth to their calves in protected areas. The newborn is well concealed within and its colour too, is well camouflaged with the dry grasses. The female parent remains in the vicinity to protect its calf. The herd remains in the near by area and the female joins the herd again, once the calf is able to accompany her.

Social Organization

Gaurs live in small herds comprising 7–12 animals. However, sometimes several such herds assemble together to form large groups. During non-mating seasons, several bulls and cows live in a herd together. Mature bulls, alone or in group, wander the adjoining areas in search of new pasture lands. The old bulls, which have lost their capacity to mate, lead permanently solitary lives. Existence of a dominance hierarchy is apparent among the Gaur bulls. The rankings are established by the size, age and threat displays, rather than actual fight. The males high up in this social hierarchy, enjoy the priviledge of mating with ripe females during breeding season. Gaur is non-territorial and shares its habitat with other members of its herd.

Threats to Survival

1. Poaching–In the past *Bos gaurus* was considered to be a species for sport hunting.
2. Cattle grazing leads to the habitat destruction and habitat alteration of these wild species.
3. This species is also very susceptible to domestic cattle diseases, such as hoof and mouth disease and Rindapest. Diseases are spread by domestic cattles that are driven into the habitat of *Bos gaurus* to graze.

Conservation Measures

Though this species is Locally Common, yet realizing the threats to its survival, this species has been listed under Schedule–I of the Wildlife (Protection) Act, 1972. Many parts of the distribution range of Gaur have been declared as protected areas in order to protect their habitat. It has also been listed as Vulnerable under the IUCN category and has already been included in the Appendix–I of the CITES. However, the major threats to this species are the habitat destruction and the spread of the Rindapest disease from domestic cattles to the wild population of Gaur. Therefore, the experts suggest that innoculation of the domestic cattles against Rindapest should be made mandatory and if possible a legal compulsion. Free innoculation facility for the cattles need to be extended to the cattle owners. Reintroduction of this species can also be considered into the areas where they were earlier reported to be present.

WILD YAK

Order: Artiodactyla

Family: Bovidae

Bos mutus **(Przewalski)**

Common Name

Dong, Brong Dong (Tibetan), *Ban Chour* (Hindi)

Present Status

Wildlife (Protection) Act, 1972	Schedule–I
IUCN	Vulnerable
CITES	Appendix–I
Local Status	Uncommon

Distribution

Worldwide Distribution

Wild Yaks were once numerous and widespread in the entire north of the Himalayas, mainly in Tibetan plateau. Currently, it is confined to remote areas of the Tibetan plateau and adjacent highlands; Gansu province of China and in the northern Ladakh of eastern Kashmir, India.

Distribution in India

In India, Wild Yakd are only found in the Chang Chenmo Valley in northern Ladakh of Kashmir. Also some reports from Satluj valley and from some of the passes of east Kumaon.

Habitat

Wild Yak is the highest dwelling animals in the world. They can survive the coldest, wildest and fiercest mountains and can withstand both arctic and desert conditions. Generally, Wild Yak occurs in treeless uplands, including plains, hills, and mountains and ranging from as low as 3200 m to about 5400 m. In alpine meadows the density is richest, but in deserts they are scarce in number and more widely dispersed. During the warmer months of the year, they remain in the permanent snow covered areas, but during winter months they migrate to the lower elevations.

Distinctive Characters

Wild Yak is a massively built animal having a drooping head, handlebar horns, humped shoulders, straight back and strong sturdy limbs which makes it a sure-footed climber. They are well adapted to highlands with dense undercoat of soft, close-matted hair, greater lung-capacity and modified blood cells. Also their thick coat and low number of sweat glands efficiently conserve heat. They can survive in temperature as low as –40°C.

The outer coat is generally dark brown to black in colour and muzzle is white. Additional warmth during severe cold is provided by the fringes of coarse hairs hanging from its flank and reaches almost to the ground and covers the chest, shoulder, thigh and lower-half of the tail. Adults are with mane formed by bushy tuft of hairs originating from in between the horns and extend upto the neck. An adult Wild Yak is about 106–180 cm in shoulder height and can weigh up to 1000 kg. Smell is their dependable sense; sight and hearing are not keenly developed.

Behavioural Biology

Wild Yaks feed mostly in the morning and evening. They travel long distances in search of food due to scarcity of vegetation; carefully following the footprints left by the lead yak. Wild Yak is very sensitive to heat and co-ordinates their seasonal movements according to the temperature and food supply. They can withstand violent winds and snowstorms for hours at a time. Like other members of the family Bovidae, they also like to bathe in water of lakes and streams, even in severe cold.

Feeding Behaviour

Wild Yak is highly gregarious. They feed on grasses, herbs, mosses and lichens. They are also reported to crunch ice or snow as a source of water, even when liquid water is available. They also lick the melting snow to meet up the requirement of water in their body. In summer months, they graze in the barren plateau. They also eat much of the 'salt-encrusted earth', generally a white crust covering the ground. Winter season requires great endurance, when many die of starvation and exposure to severe cold.

Reproductive Behaviour

Generally mating occurs in the month of September. Gestation period is approximately 260 days. Most births occur from April through June.Probably they give birth to single calf in alternate years, but in areas with scanty vegetation, one may give birth only once in every three years. Generally the youngs become independent at one year of age and become sexually mature at around 3–4 years and attain their full-grown size at 6–8 years of age. They can survive upto 23 years.

Social Organization

Females and youngs congregate in large herds upto 100 or more individuals. It was reported that sometimes a single herd contains thousands of individuals. These herds are not stable units, may readily split or someone can join the herd at any time. The adult males generally remain solitary throughout the year and join the herd at the time of rutting.

Threats to Survival

1. Uncontrolled hunting by natives and military personnel has reduced their number by more than half during the last century.
2. This species was also reported to be killed for the wool and tail tuft which were being traded.
3. Habitat loss and degradation of habitat. Wild Yak has lost most of the best alpine meadow and steppe habitat.
4. Hybridization with domestic yaks.
5. Competition with domestic yaks.
6. Disease transmitted by domestic yaks.

Conservation Measures

According to IUCN, Wild Yak is designated as Vulnerable, its local status is Uncommon and it is placed in the Schedule–I of Wildlife (Protection) Act, 1972, providing the animal legal protection. Ban was imposed on the international trade on any of their body parts through their inclusion in the Appendix–I of CITES.

To increase the population size of this species, experts suggest that captive breeding programme could be initiated and if found successful, the new animals can be planned to be reintroduced in the areas of its distribution range.

ASIATIC WILD ASS

Order: Perissodactyla

Family: Equidae

***Equus onager khur* (Lesson)**

Common Name

Ghor khar (Gujarati); *Khur* (Hindi)

Present Status

Wildlife (Protection) Act, 1972	Schedule–I
IUCN	Vulnerable
CITES	Appendix–I
Local Status	Locally common

Distribution

Worldwide Distribution

Equus onager was found from Mongolia to Saudi Arabia and as far north as southern Russia and Kazakhstan. Some also inhabited northwestern India and Tibet. However, at present, Asiatic Wild Ass is confined to India only.

Distribution in India

Asiatic Wild Ass is distributed in the Rann of Kutch in the state of Gujarat. It is best seen at Dhrangadhara Wildlife Sanctuary in Gujarat.

Habitat

It inhabits flat arid regions. It prefers habitats with salt encrusted soils, sterile countryside with grasses, scrubs and xerophytic vegetations of low height. They are attracted by the flat and grass covered stretches, known as 'bets'. These bets are the patches of coarse grasses that sprout vigorously with the monsoon inundations.

Distinctive Characters

Asiatic Wild Ass is smaller than a horse but larger than the domestic ass. The coat colour varies from reddish-grey to pale chestnut. Under parts and abdomen are pale and white in colour. They have a fringe of hair on its neck. This hair continues in the form of a thin dark stripe from mane to tail. Stallions are marginally larger than the mares. However, this difference cannot be distinguished easily. They weigh around 250–300 kg and measures 100–120 cm at shoulder.

Behavioural Biology

Asiatic Wild Ass is a terrestrial animal with cursorial adaptation. They can gallop at an average speed of 30–35 km/hr, which at times may reach up to 50 km/hr. It has got an excellent sense of smell. During daytimes, they remain inactive and are found in small or large parties of 10–30 individuals. Asiatic Wild Asses are social animals and the entire group stays together except in the foaling season when the mares and the foals stay separate from the stallions.

Feeding Behaviour

Asiatic Wild Asses are completely herbivorous in nature. They feed on the xerophytic plants, grasses and other scrubs that grow in their habitat. They feed in early morning and late afternoon. They also raid the cultivations at night. During the rainy season, the herds forage at the higher and drier areas of the bets and foraging freely from one patch to another. However, during the dry seasons, when the grasses of these bets wither, they shift to other bets near the perennial supply of water and with some green grasses.

Reproductive Behaviour

Mating of Asiatic Wild Ass was reported to take place between August–October. The stallions fight with the other stallions to take possession of a mare in heat. Then they separate from the troop and mate. After a period of isolation, the couple joins the group. Then the female actively resists advances by other males. The gestation period is about 11 months. At the end of the gestation period, one foal is born generally between July–September. Both the sexes live separately until the foal is about three months old. The maximum life span is reported to be approximately forty years.

Social Organization

E. onager usually lives in herds, with the exception of older stallions, which can be found living in solitude. Mares live with their foals in herds made up entirely of other females and youngs. Herd size may vary; average herds contain between 10 and 20 animals, with one male and many females. A dominant stallion usually mates with females in the herd. In order to assure breeding status, stallions defend the territories that females move through and the best territories are usually defended by the dominant stallions.

Threats to Survival

1. Habitat disturbance and loss of habitat.
2. Competition for food and water with livestocks.
3. Surrah disease which is being spread to the Asiatic Wild Ass from the domestic animals.
4. Hunted by humans in the past for their flesh and hides.

Conservation Measures

E. onager has been listed as Vulnerable by the IUCN. It has been reported that there are at present less than 1000 individuals surviving in the wild. However, there were reports of 3000–5000 individuals of Asiatic Wild Ass in the year 1946. This population size sharply reduced from 4000 in 1956 (Wyner Blyth, 1956) to 870 in 1962 (Gee, 1964) and 368 in 1969 (Schaller and Simon, 1970). The census by the Gujrat Forest Department during 1976 revealed a population size of 720 individuals. Realizing this grave situation it has been brought under the Schedule–I of the Wildlife (Protection) Act, 1972, which give them the highest degree of legal protection. This species has also been brought under the Appendix–I of the CITES preventing any of its part being used for trade. The major distribution range of the Asiatic Wild Ass around the Runn of Kutch in Gujarat has been protected as Dhrangadhara Wildlife Sanctuary. However, experts suggest that the domestic cattles should be vaccinated to prevent the spread of disease to the population of the Asiatic Wild Ass and the reclamation and cultivation in marshland should also be stopped.

SLOTH BEAR

Order: Carnivora

Family: Ursidae

***Melursus ursinus* (Shaw)**

Common Name

Bhalu, Reech, Rinch (Hindi); *Asval* (Marathi); *Elugu bunti* (Telugu); *Puni karadi* (Malayali); *Karadi* (Tamil, Kannar); *Bhalluk* (Bengali)

Present Status

Wildlife (Protection) Act, 1972	Schedule I
IUCN	Vulnerable
CITES	Appendix–I
Local Status	Locally common

Distribution

Worldwide Distribution

Most Sloth Bears live in India and Sri Lanka. It is also found in southern Nepal, Bhutan and Bangladesh.

Distribution in India

Sloth Bear is distributed throughout India in tropical and subtropical forests except Jammu and Kashmir, high Himalayas. There is no report of their occurrence in arid and desert areas of Gujarat and Rajasthan.

Habitat

Sloth Bear prefers the scrub, deciduous forests and grasslands. It inhabits the rocky terrains inside the forests with a perennial water source. Sloth Bears mainly prefer the dense forests of sal, mahua, teak, margosa, mango, fig and bamboo in the tropical and sub-tropical forests.

Distinctive Characters

Sloth Bears grow 140–170 cm in length, stand 65–85 cm at shoulder and weigh 65–145 kg. They have shaggy, dusty black coat, short hind legs, pale and yellowish muzzle and long curved claws which are used to excavate ants and termites. A cream-coloured "V" shaped mark is present on their chest. Nostrils of Sloth Bear can close, protecting the animal from dust or insects when raiding termite nests or bee-hives. A gap in the teeth, due to lack of front incisors, enables them to suck up ants, termites and other insects.

The sexual dimorphism is not so distinct in Sloth Bears. The males possess scrotal sacs and are bigger than the females. During breeding season, conspicuous mammary gland is distinct in the females. Sloth bears have a potential life span of 40 years, but they generally do not reach this age in the wild.

Behavioural Biology

Sloth Bears are generally nocturnal in habit. However, in a cool and cloudy day, they are less rigidly nocturnal and are found to be active even during the daytime. They are noisy and busy animals. It grunts and snorts as it pulls down branches to get fruits or dig the termite mounds or snuffles under debris for grubs and beetles. The Sloth Bear is dim-sighted and rears up on its hind legs and bites or claws when alarmed.

Sloth Bear cubs are born in an underground den and stay there for several months. Females remain inside the den protecting the cubs for 2–3 months and rarely come out to feed. The cubs, when sufficiently strong to grip, are carried to and from the feeding grounds on their mother's back. During this time the female parent is very aggressive to ensure defense for her cubs. The cubs stay with their mother for another two to three years until they become completely independent.

Feeding Behaviour

They become active shortly before sunset, start searching for food throughout the night and retire in the morning. Sloth Bears are omnivorous animals. Their food depends upon locality and season. Usually feed on fruits, specially mango, fig, ebony and other fruits and also on some flowers. Occationally they raid the crop fields, mainly maize and sugarcane fields when the crops are in the ripe condition. The Sloth Bears are good climbers and they climb trees to knock down honey-combs and to collect honey from the comb. During the monsoons, they feed on insects in the forest areas, under stones and fallen logs, under barks and in the crevices of the trees. Beetles, grubs, ants and other insects, especially termites form the major part of their diet. In the scarcity of these foods in the wild, Sloth Bear is also reported to feed on carrion.

Reproductive Behaviour

During their breeding season, groups of three to four males congregate near estrous females and give out a long and melodious mating call. They are particularly noisy during mating, which generally occur during hot summer. Males breed with the females apparently in ranked order and the same order of breeding hierarchy is usually followed among the same group of males while mating with different females. Gestation period varies between six and seven months and the females usually give birth to two cubs between December and January.

Social Organization

Sloth Bears usually lead a solitary life except for the breeding season and while accompanied by the young. The males leave the females soon after mating is over and the females are responsible for providing parental care for the young. The cubs stay with their mother till they are two to three years old and food collections are accompanied by their mother. During this time the mother bear is most aggressive and communicate with their young using a specific call. Once they reach maturity they leave their mother and switch on to the solitary mode of life.

Threats to Survival

1. Destruction of the habitats of these animals due to extension of human settlements and agricultural lands, construction of roads and illegal logging.
2. Poaching of the animals for their hide, skin and gall bladder. Bear bile is widely used in the Tibetan medicine and also in several folk medicines in the northeastern India. To meet the large-scale demand of bear bile, often sloth bears are killed to collect their gall bladders.
3. Often adult bears are killed or trapped and the cubs are captured by the *madaris* and cubs are then trained for the "Dancing Bear Trade". These performing bears die at a young age due to malnutrition, mishandling and several diseases.
4. Several diseases in the wild.
5. Leopards, tigers and other large predators kill Sloth Bears, especially the bear cubs.
6. Natural calamities like drought, earthquake and fire also affect Sloth Bear population in the wild.

Conservation Measures

Sloth Bear is legally protected under the Wildlife (Protection) Act, 1972 and is a Schedule–I species. Though Locally Common, yet considering the threats to its survival IUCN has categorized this species as Vulnerable. Realizing its threat from the bear bile trade, this species has been placed under Appendix–I of CITES which altogether prohibits the trade of any part of these animals. Several protected areas have been declared in its distribution range to protect its habitat as well as the animal from poaching and other threats to their survival. Wildlife Trust of India, has presently undertaken a comprehensive project to conserve Sloth Bear throughout its distribution range in India. Awareness campaigns among the locals as well as among the *madaris* involved in the "Dancing Bear Trade" is necessary and a conservation strategy through community participation could be evolved for better conservation of the Sloth Bears.

CLOUDED LEOPARD

Order: Carnivora

Family: Felidae

***Neofelis nebulosa* (Griffith)**

Common Name

Kung (Bhotia); *Pungmar, Satchuk* (Lepcha); *Amchita* (Nepali); *Thit kyoung* (Burmese); *Godaphutki bagh* (Assamese); *Kelral* (Mizo); *Lamchita* (Bengali)

Present Status

Wildlife (Protection) Act, 1972	Schedule–I
IUCN	Vulnerable
CITES	Appendix–I
Local Status	Rare

Distribution

Worldwide Distribution

Clouded Leopard is found in northeastern parts of India. It has also been reported from Nepal, Bhutan, Myanmar extending towards northeast to southern China and southeastward to Indonesia and Malaysia.

Distribution in India

It is distributed in northern parts of West Bengal, Sikkim, Assam and eastward to the other northeastern states.

Habitat

Clouded Leopards inhabit dense evergreen forests. They prefer tropical rain forests with dense vegetation cover, large trees and dense undergrowth. They ambush prey sitting on the tree trunks.

Distinctive Characters

The coat colour of the Clouded Leopard varies from greenish to earthy-brown to rich yellowish brown with white/pale under parts. On the coat gray elliptical cloudy spots edged with black are present, which turn into blurred rings on its long tail. Its face is marked with usual cheek stripes and the head is spotted. Two broad bands on its neck run more or less regularly to the hinder part of their body. The back of each ear is black with a gray spot in the middle. Total body length of a Clouded Leopard varies from 60–110 cm and weighs around 11–20 kg. Clouded Leopard is the smallest of the big cats found in India. It has the longest canine among the felids as compared to the skull size.

Behavioural Biology

Clouded Leopard is arboreal in nature and leads a nocturnal mode of life. They do not leave scats and scraps along its trail. They are generally solitary. It can hang from tree branches by its hind leg and tail and can climb down the tree trunks in a 'head-down' posture.

Feeding Behaviour

They are carnivorous in nature and feed on deers, antelopes, birds, small rodents and small reptiles. Sometimes they visit forest villages inside their habitat to prey upon domestic animals like goats, pigs and poultries.

Reproductive Behaviour

Females give birth to a litter of 1–5 cubs after a gestation period of about 85 to 93 days. The newborns are blind and helpless and instead of dark rings in adults, the kittens' spots are completely dark. They are able to see within ten days of birth and are active within five weeks. They become independent at about ten months of age. The Clouded Leopards reach sexual maturity at two years of age and females are able to bear one litter each year. In the wild, they have an average life span of 11 years. While in captivity, they may live as long as 17 years. Males and females unite only during the mating season. It usually hides its young in the hollow of a tree.

Social Organization

Clouded Leopards usually lead a solitary life and only during the breeding season the male pairs with a receptive female. They are very secretive in nature and are rarely seen in the wild. Once the breeding is over, they isolate. The females accompany and protect the cubs until they become completely mature and independent.

Threats to Survival

1. Poaching of this animal is done mainly for their skin. Clouded Leopards have been hunted for the fur trade and for their body parts which are

supposed to have medicinal properties. These animals were hunted mainly for its striking pelt, teeth and bones.

2. Habitat loss and habitat fragmentation: Many areas within their distribution range have been converted into agricultural lands and for many other developmental activities. Its habitat is also being destroyed through logging as well as by advancing human settlements.

Conservation Measures

According to IUCN, Clouded Leopard is designated as Vulnerable due to overhunting and deforestation and its local status is Rare. It is placed in the Schedule–I of Wildlife (Protection) Act, 1972, thus protected from any illegal killing of the animal. At present 1000 km2 of its distribution range has been notified as protected areas in Sikkim, Meghalaya and Arunachal Pradesh. Being in the Appendix–I of CITES, prevent any part of it from being used in international trade. Literatures suggest that, captive breeding programmes have been attempted, but so far they have been unsuccessful due to the small gene pool available in captivity, as well as in the wild individuals.

Extensive field surveys need to be conducted to evaluate the present population status, distribution range, feeding behaviour and habitat condition of Clouded Leopard. This in turn, will help in determining the conservation and management strategies for this species. Experts suggest that the areas of the existing sanctuaries at Meghalaya, especially in the Garo hills, need to be enlarged.

GOLDEN CAT

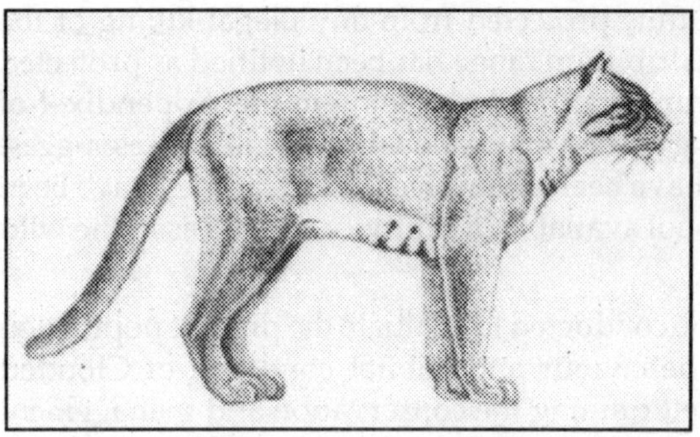

Order: Carnivora

Family: Felidae

Catopuma temminckii
(Vigors and Horsfield)

Common Name

Tokpa (Manipuri); *Shonali mekuri* (Assamese); *Shonali biral* (Bengali)

Present Status

Wildlife (Protection) Act, 1972	Schedule–I
IUCN	Vulnerable
CITES	Appendix–I
Local Status	Rare

Distribution

Worldwide Distribution

Golden Cat is found in India, Nepal, Bhutan, south China and southeast Asia extending as far south as Indonesia.

Distribution in India

In India, this species is distributed in Sikkim, Assam and in parts of other northeastern states.

Habitat

Golden Cat prefers tropical and subtropical moist deciduous and evergreen forests. It lives in the plain lands and also prefers rocky terrains.

Distinctive Characters

Golden Cat is largest of the group of lesser cats measuring over 120 cm in total length and weighing 6–11 kg. Coat colour of the animal varies from golden brown, dark brown, bright red to gray. Coat is short, smooth and is devoid of any pattern of colouration. However, cats with black coloured coat or marbled pattern are also recorded. A conspicuous horizontal white or buff cheek stripe, sometimes edged with black, is present in the inner rims of eyes and a white line on the bottom of the tail.

Behavioural Biology

This medium sized cat leads a nocturnal mode of life. During daytime, they take refuge in the hollow tree trunk or between crevices of the rock in their habitat. During dusk, they roam inside the forest in search of food. These animals are solitary in nature. They seldom take to the trees for safety. Individuals do not display the fierceness as is ascribed to this species.

Feeding Behaviour

They are carnivorous in nature and feed on wild hares, small deers, antelopes, birds, small rodents and lizards. Sometimes they visit forest villages inside their habitat to prey upon domestic animals like goats, pigs and poultries.

Reproductive Behaviour

They are very secretive in nature and breeding takes place in hollow trees, among rocks or in hollows in the ground. Females have an estrous period of six days and the entire estrous cycle is completed in 39 days. Gestation period lasts for around 95 days after which they produce a litter of one to two kittens. The kittens weigh about 250 g at birth. After birth their body weight quickly increases and the kittens double their weight at 3 weeks and triple it by 6 weeks. There is apparently no specific breeding season and if one litter is dead another will be produced within 4 months. Females reach sexual maturity within 18–24 months while males reach sexual maturity at the age of two years.

Social Organization

Very little is known about its social behaviour. Like all other cats they are also supposed to lead a solitary life. Only during the breeding season, the male pairs with a receptive female. They are very secretive in nature and are rarely seen in the wild. It was reported that the males play an active role in rearing youngs. The females accompany and protect the cubs until they become completely mature and independent.

Threats to Survival

1. Poaching of this animal is done mainly for their skin. Their pelts and bones are also traded.
2. Golden cats are also reported to be used as a source of food by several tribal groups within its distribution range in the northeastern India.

3. Areas within their distribution range have been converted into agricultural lands and for many other developmental activities leading to habitat loss and habitat fragmentation.

Conservation Measures

According to IUCN status, Golden Cat is designated as Vulnerable and its local status is Rare. Considering the threats to its survival, it is placed under Schedule–I of Wildlife (Protection) Act, 1972 providing the animal with a nationwide legal protection. Several protected areas have been declared within its distribution range. Being in the Appendix–I of CITES, prevent any part of it from being used in international trade.

In spite of all these conservation measures, it is believed that their population is declining. Countrywide population census of Golden Cat is to be done. It is also necessary to identify their habitat especially their breeding grounds. Once identified, these habitats need to be protected from poaching, destruction due to several anthropogenic activities and from other conservation threats.

FISHING CAT

Order: Carnivora

Family: Felidae

***Prionailurus viverrinus* (Bennett)**

Common Name

Fishing cat (English), *Mechho biral* (Bengali)

Present Status

Wildlife (Protection) Act, 1972	Schedule–I
IUCN	Vulnerable
CITES	Appendix–II
Local Status	Uncommon

Distribution

Worldwide Distribution

Fishing Cats are found in many places throughout Asia. It occurs in Sri Lanka, Pakistan, Nepal, Bhutan, Bangladesh, from Myanmar to Vietnam, Malaysia, Indonesia, South China and India.

Distribution in India

In India, it is found in parts of West Bengal, Uttar Pradesh, Keonjhar district and vicinity of Chilika Lake in Orissa, from Mangalore to Kanyakumari in the west coast.

Habitat

Fishing Cats live primarily in wetland areas in the marshes as well as, in the swamps. It is frequently found in the grass swamps or in the reed beds adjacent to the rivers and tidal creeks. They are also reported to live in heavily forested regions adjacent to rivers or near jungles. It inhabits the forests up to 1525 m in the Himalayas and also in the swamps at the base of these mountains.

Distinctive Characters

Fishing Cat is an elongated, medium sized, stout animal with characteristic short limbs. The head and body together measures about 100 cm, the tail is about 30 cm in length and weighs 11–15 kg. The tail has markings with incomplete dark rings and has a black tip. Its coat is short and coarse and is blackish brown in colour. The short and blunt ears on either side of the head are black on the outer side with a white spot. Six to eight black lines run down from the forehead to the neck. Blackish brown cheek stripes are also present. The blackish brown body markings consist of elongated spots arranged in longitudinal rows.

Sexual dimorphism is very distinct in Fishing Cats. The body size and the whiskers of the males are much bigger than that of the females. The presence of scrotal sac in male is another distinguishing character. During the breeding season, conspicuous mammary glands are distinct in females. The mammary gland is found along the ventro-lateral side of the body from the axilla to the groin.

Behavioural Biology

Fishing Cats are semiarboreal and predatory in nature. During daytime it remains hidden in the bushes and the branches of the trees. Fishing Cat is generally found to come out of its den in the late afternoon or in the evening. However, this animal rarely comes out during the daytime. It becomes active in the night as it has the nocturnal mode of life. This animal prefers to stay in the dark and shaded places.

Feeding Behaviour

These animals fed on the freshly killed animals and fishes. Fishes are favourite food for these animals. They never feed on stale meat and fishes. However, Fishing Cats sometime feed on molluscs and the meat of calves and goats. It predates fishes and other molluscs from the swamp regions of the forests. Its fishing strategy is to crouch on a rock or overhanging bank and to scoop up the fish with a blow of its paw. It generally does not enter the water to predate on its prey. It starts feeding from the head of the animal it is feeding on. Reports suggest that the amount of food consumed by a fishing cat is 1–1.5 kg of fish daily.

Reproductive Behaviour

Very little is known about the breeding biology of Fishing Cats in the wild. Fishing Cats are polyestrous animals and are found to breed throughout the year.

The estrous cycle lasts for 21–25 days approximately. It has been found that the females become receptive at the middle of the estrous cycle. Then they become restless and are occasionally found to roll on the ground. Frequent micturation is also found during this period.

Social Organization

There is little available information on social behaviour of Fishing Cats. They are usually solitary in nature and do not lead a social life. The adult males only couple with the receptive females at the time of breeding. The females play a major role in caring the youngs. The young cubs are accompanied by their mother until they become completely mature and independent.

Threats to Survival

1. Destruction of the habitats of these animals is taking place due to extension of human settlements and agricultural lands, construction of roads and illegal logging. The major threat to Fishing Cats is the destruction of their habitat, primarily wetlands. For example, in Sri Lanka it has been documented that a variety of factors are responsible for the loss of habitat, including land reclamation, dumping, clearing of the natural vegetation, and pollution.
2. Fishing Cats are in danger due to destructive fishing practices that greatly reduce the fish stock. Fisherman communities often consider these animals as pests.
3. Poaching of these animals for their hide and skin. They are often hunted for food, medicine or various body parts.
4. Parasitic diseases are often found to kill a large number of these animals.
5. Periodic floods are also a cause of their dwindling population.

Conservation Measures

Fishing Fishing Cat is legally protected under the Wildlife (Protection) Act, 1972, and is a Schedule–I species. Therefore, the law prohibits the hunting and killing of this species throughout the country. Being in the Appendix–II of CITES, it is strictly protected from trade. According to IUCN, the status of Fishing Cat is designated as Vulnerable and it is locally Uncommon. There are reports that the species is marginally benefited by improved protection in the conservation areas of Rajasthan and Gujarat. The total conservation cover for this species is about 10,000 km^2.

The population of this species is supposed to be declining. To identify the habitat and breeding grounds of the Fishing Cats, extensive field surveys need to be planned and these habitats need to be protected from poaching, destruction due to several anthropogenic activities and from other conservation threats. Areas with healthy population of Fishing Cats outside the protected areas need to be conserved through awareness generation and community participation.

INDIAN GIANT SQUIRREL

Order: Rodentia

Family: Sciuridae

***Ratufa indica* (Erxleben)**

Common Name

Karat, Rasu, Jangli gilheri (Hindi); *Anil, Betudata* (Tamil); *Malayannan* (Malayalam); *Keshalilu, Kesannalu* (Kannada); *Shekru* (Marathi); *Sekut* (Gujarati).

Present Status

Wildlife (Protection) Act, 1972	Schedule–I
IUCN	Vulnerable
CITES	Appendix–II
Local Status	Rare

Distribution

Worldwide Distribution

The distribution of *Ratufa indica* is restricted to peninsular India.

Distribution in India

Different subspecies of Indian Giant Squirrels are found in most part of peninsular India in the south, mainly in the region of Western Ghats. An isolated population of Indian Giant Squirrel is found in the northeastern India upto south of Jharkhand. Indian Giant Squirrel is best seen at the Periyar National Park in Kerala.

Habitat

It prefers mixed deciduous and evergreen forests south of 22°N. They mostly stay at the canopy layer of the trees and seldom come down to ground. They have mastered arboreal adaptation and move from tree to tree taking leaps with outspread limbs. They are found in the deciduous, mixed deciduous and moist evergreen forests in the plains as well as in the hills.

Distinctive Characters

Indian Giant Squirrel is an endemic mammal with varying degree of bright-pelages in different geographical races. Their ventral coat colour is creamay buff. The race found in the northern Western Ghats is brownish maroon in appearance dorsally with a complete brown or brown and white tail, whereas in the south it is black and dark maroon with a tail intermingled with black and brown. On the other hand, the central and south-east Indian races are brown dorsally with black forelegs and a black tail with a pale tip. Head to body length of Indian Giant Squirrel varies from 35–50 cm and the tail is around 60 cm long.

Behavioural Biology

Indian Giant Squirrel has adapted to arboreal mode of life and is diurnal in nature. They are active and agile animals and remain most active during the early hours in the morning and in the evening. During mid-day they take rest and retire to their refuge. It sleeps on the tree branches spreading their hind and forelegs wide apart and holding the branch, whereas, its long tail hangs downward from the branch. However, during winter and rainy season they take shelter inside the nests.

Feeding Behaviour

Very little is known about the feeding behaviour of these animals. They are believed to be strictly vegetarian in nature. Their food comprises of several fruits, nuts and leaves. They forage mainly during the day time and sleep on the tree trunks or nests at night.

Reproductive Behaviour

Very little is known about the mating behaviour *Ratufa indica.* Males actively compete for females during the breeding season and pairs may remain associated for longer periods of time. There are reports that breeding occurs throughout the year or several times during the year. Litter size is usually one or two young, but may be as many as three. Gestation period in a close relative, *Ratufa bicolor*, was recorded to be 28 to 35 days.

Social Organization

Indian Giant Squirrels are typically solitary animals, being seen only rarely in pairs during the breeding season. They usually take shelter in the nests during winter and rainy seasons when the weather is harsh. They prepare globular nests using leaves and tree twigs on the tiny tree branches to avoid heavier predators. They make several nests. Separate nests are used for resting, nursing the young ones etc. The brilliantly coloured creatures are more heard than seen and it is not easy to locate them in the wild due to their secretive and wary nature. However, their loud repeated rattling calls reveal their presence. They give alarm calls at any unusual sighting.

Threats to Survival

1. Habitat loss and habitat destruction due to reckless deforestation has further reduced the habitat of *R. indica* which was already fragmented and reduced due to several anthropogenic activities.
2. Poaching for their pelt.

Conservation Measures

IUCN has listed the Indian Giant Squirrel as Endangered and considering its threats to survival, this species has been listed under the Schedule–I of the Wildlife (Protection) Act, 1972. Therefore, the killing of this species is prohibited and is punishable under law. It has also been brought under the Appendix–II of CITES as *Ratufa* sp. Several areas within its distribution range have already been declared as protected areas. Agencies such as the IUCN and CITES have acted to reduce their chance of extinction and any further fragmentation of their habitat.

NEAR THREATENED AND LOWER RISK

INDIAN ANTELOPE or BLACKBUCK

Order: Artiodactyla

Family: Bovidae

***Antilope cervicapra* (Linnaeus)**

Common Name

Krishnashar (Bengali), *Barat* (Nepali), *Moorukoo* (Tamil), *Chigri* (Kannad), *Ladijinka* (Telugu), *Mrig* (Hindi)

Present Status

Wildlife (Protection) Act, 1972	Schedule–I
IUCN	Near Threatened
CITES	Appendix–III
Local Status:	Common

Distribution

Worldwide Distribution

Blackbuck is found in Pakistan, Nepal and India.

Distribution in India

Blackbuck occurs throughout the Indian plains except the northeast, the eastern limit being Chilika Lake in Orissa and in the south it is distributed till Point Calimere, Tamil Nadu. It is, however, not reported from the Malabar coast. It is quite abundant in Rajasthan, Punjab, Haryana, Gujarat and parts of central India.

Habitat

Its original habitat is open plain and not dense jungles. On the open plains, Blackbuck is one of the fastest animals and can outrun most predators over long distances.

Distinctive Characters

Male Blackbuck has a blackish brown or an almost black coat with white underparts. Inside of the legs, the lower third of each flank, the chin, a patch around the eyes and inner side of the ears are white. It measures 120–130 cm in head and body length and 17–18 cm in the length of the tail, whereas standing height is about 80 cm at the shoulder. An adult Blackbuck weighs around 32–43 kg.

The females are smaller with yellowish fawn above and white below and are invariably hornless. The male, however, possess a pair of spirally twisted closely ringed horns, which are about 40–50 cm in length.

Behavioural Biology

Blackbucks in the wild are usually seen in herds of 10 to 30 or even over 100 individuals. It prefers flat open ground covered with grasses, bushes and scrubs but avoids forests and hilly tracts. It is said to be one of the fastest animals in the world and can reach to a speed of 100–140 km per hour. When alarmed, it moves off in a series of leaps and bounds. Each herd has a master buck, which may live in company with as many as fifty or more.

They are generally seen throughout the day in herds during the winter season. In contrary, during summer, they are active in the very early morning and late afternoon and rest in the shade at other times to avoid excessive heat and scorching sun. Blackbucks are very shy and wary. Their sense of smell and hearing are not highly developed so they rely on eyesight in detecting danger. They are usually silent, but sometimes females give a hissing noise that warns the herd of danger. When in danger, a single animal bounds in the air and is soon followed by the rest of the herd. These animals have great speed and endurance; when in danger they can maintain a gallop with a speed of 40 miles/hr for approximately 15 miles.

Feeding Behaviour

Blackbucks feed largely on grasses, weak-stemmed plants, scrubs of *Acacia* sp., fruits and other vegetations like cultivated grains. They consume very little amount of water. Studying their drinking habits, T.J. Roberts writes, "It has been reliably established that they do not drink water even when it is available. It may be that they can recirculate the nitrogen in their bodies rather than having to excrete it in their urine." This mode of conserving and ability to recirculate water has helped them to adapt in the dry and xeric conditions of their habitat.

Reproductive Behaviour

The rutting season is in the spring or winter. Although breeding can occur throughout the year, there are peak periods in March–May and August–October. During the rut, the mature males establish a territory by regularly depositing faeces in particular points. Males are extremely aggressive during this time and drive all other males from their territory by a throaty grunt and an occasional horn fight. The gestation period is about six months and most of the time a single young is born. The young is able to run about soon after birth.

Social Organization

Blackbucks are gregarious and social animals. They live in herds generally ranging from 5 to 50 individuals. The herds are actually harem of a single adult male with a number of adult females and their youngs.

Threats to Survival

Hunting and Poaching

It was prized for its meat and was considered as a sporting trophy.

Habitat Destruction

Decimation of its population has been accelerated due to rapid agro–industrial development in its preferred habitation throughout the country (Schallar, 1967).

Conservation Measures

Though it is Locally Common, IUCN has listed this antelope as Near Threatened considering its global population status and considering its present threats. It is also placed in the Schedule–I of Wildlife (Protection) Act, 1972, thus providing them a nationwide legal protection. Several protected areas have been declared within its habitat to protect this species as well as to safeguard its habitat. Blackbuck was once the most abundant among the hoofed mammals in India and Pakistan, but their populations have been greatly reduced through excessive hunting and loss of habitat due to agricultural development.

BLUE SHEEP or BHARAL

Order: Artiodactyla

Family: Bovidae

***Pseudois nayaur* (Hodgson)**

Common Name

Bharal, Bharar, Bharut (Hindi); *Sna, Na* (Ladakhi); *Nao* (Bhutia); *Nervaati* (Nepali)

Present Status

Wildlife (Protection) Act, 1972	Schedule–I
IUCN	Lower Risk
CITES	No Special Status
Local Status	Locally common

Distribution

Worldwide Distribution

This animal is found mostly in Tibet. However, it is also found in Ladakh, Kumaon Himalayas, Nepal, Sikkim and Bhutan.

Distribution in India

In India, they are found in parts of Jammu and Kashmir, Himachal Pradesh, Uttaranchal, Sikkim and northeast India.

Habitat

Bharal is found in the open grass areas and high mountain cliffs in the alpine zones above the tree lines. They inhabit at an altitude of 4880 m in summer and 3660 m in winter. They never enter forests or scrub lands and prefer open lands with abundance of food.

Distinctive Characters

The animal is 90 cm at shoulder and weighing about 55 to 70 kg. The general coat colour of head and dorsal surface is brownish grey. The face and chest of the adult males are black and a black stripe runs along the middle of each flank till the down of the legs. In females, all these black markings are absent. During winter, this colouration becomes more prominent while in summer the coat becomes red-brown for better camouflage. Its horns are rounded, smooth and backwardly curved over its neck. Horns are olive black in colour and measure about 60 cm in length. It has no facial glands and lack any beard. However, feet glands are present between hooves in all four feet.

Behavioural Biology

Bharals show a mixture of goat and sheep traits. They graze on open undulating lands and also climb efficiently to the alpine cliffs and when disturbed even ascend to the most difficult and inaccessible places. They are diurnal in nature and feed and rest alternatively during daytime. While resting, they lie down on the feeding ground and make them indistinguishable from their surroundings. Like goats, they mouth their own red penis as threat display and make a squirrel like 'chirrt' alarm call. They rub their mouth in their rivals back as a sign of appeasement like sheep.

Feeding Behaviour

Bharals are strictly vegetarian in nature. They feed on grasses, mosses and dwarf shrubs. They also feed on few fungal species present in the alpine regions.

Reproductive Behaviour

Their rutting season commences during September. The large flocks of *Bharals* break into small groups during this time. Each small groups consist of a ram and his harem of females accompanied by few immature males. During rutting season, males rear up and strike each other like goats. However, during courtship male *Bharals* raise their forelegs and stretch out their head in a sheep-like fashion.

Social Organization

Males are generally solitary or sometimes found together in a group of 4–5, while females and youngs are found in groups. In summer, they are found in herds of 10–50 animals, whereas during winter the number raises as high as 200.

Threats to Survival

1. Destruction of the habitats due to cattle grazing by the shepherds in the alpine meadows.
2. Poaching of the animals for their hide, skin and horn.

Conservation Measures

Bharal is placed in the Schedule–I of Wildlife (Protection) Act, 1972, thus giving a countrywide protection. Several protected areas have been declared in its distribution range to protect its habitat as well as the animal from poaching. In India, these animals are best seen at the Nanda Devi National Park at Uttaranchal.

HIMALAYAN MUSK DEER

Order: Artiodactyla

Family: Moschidae

***Moschus chrysogaster* (Hodgson)**

The taxonomy of these animals is rather disputed. Some taxonomists suggest the presence of only one species (*M. moschiferus*) with several subspecies. Flerov (1928) suggests 3 species namely–*M. moschiferus* (Siberian), *M. chrysogaster* (Himalayan) and *M. berezovaskii* (Chinese). However, Groves (1975) recognized 2 species from India–*M. chrysogaster* (Alpine) and *M. sifanicus* (forest belt)

Common Name

Kosturi horin (Assamese), *Hodung, Sibuei, Sikung* (Adi), *Garawa, Loh* (Monpa), *Kastura, Mushk* (Hindi), *Roos* (%), *Roos-kutt* (&) (Kashmiri)

Present Status

Wildlife (Protection) Act, 1972	Schedule–I
IUCN	Lower Risk
CITES	Appendix–I
Local Status	Uncommon

Distribution

Worldwide Distribution

Musk Deers range over a wide geographical area including at least thirteen countries of Asia and Russia. They are mainly distributed throughout the southern slope of Himalayas; India, Pakistan, Nepal, China, Bhutan, Tibet, Myanmar, Korea, Russia and Vietnam.

Distribution in India

In India, Musk Deers are found in Jammu and Kashmir, Himachal Pradesh, Uttar Pradesh, Uttaranchal, Sikkim and Arunachal Pradesh.

Habitat

Musk Deers prefer rugged terrains ranging between 2200–4000 m altitudes. It occupies both alpine and forest belt and are generally found within birch forest above the zone of pine forest. Rock outcrops are generally the favourite habitats for the Himalayan Musk Deers which also provide them shelter from predators.

Distinctive Characters

Musk Deers are placed between the deers and the antelopes and are regarded as undeveloped form of deer, without horns and facial glands. They are unique in having gall bladder, which no other deer possesses. In males, the upper canines are long extending below the upper lip. The ears are large and rounded. Hindlegs are long and well muscled, while forelegs are shorter and weak and rump is higher than shoulders. Body coat possess long hairs, rich dark brown in colour and speckled with white on the flanks and white stocking legs. Age related changes in hair coats and colour could be noticed. New borns possess dark brown coat with short and soft hairs densely covered with yellowish or white spots. In winter, spots become less pronounced. Tail is short and completely buried in the long hairs of the anal region. Males possess musk gland, anterior to male genitals. Fresh musk gland secretion has an unpleasant, pungent, urinary smell; but after becoming dry it acquires the scent of musk. Head and body length is about 80-100 cm, height at shoulder is 50–70 cm and weight between 13–18 kg. Musk Deer is also recognized by distinctive jumping movement like kangaroo.

Behavioural Biology

Musk Deers are most active at twilight or at night. They are generally shy and secretive animals. Their vision and hearing are keen but the sense of smell is poor. They often move solitary and are highly territorial or are found in groups of 2–3. Musk pouch releases a scent to attract mate. During the rutting season in winter, male Musk Deers fight each other for the receptive female and during the process cut deep slashes on rivals with their long canines. They are also reported to migrate from steep mountains to grassy meadows near river valley, specially in winter.

Feeding Behaviour

Musk Deers feed on grasses, herbs, mosses, ferns and lichens. In winter, they generally depend upon arboreal lichens, terrestrial bushy lichens (70 per cent) for food and also eat young shoots, coniferous needles, leave buds and barks. During summer, they eat herbaceous plants.

Reproductive Behaviour

The females attain sexual maturity within 16–17 months and males after 2–3 years. Females are reported to be in the estrous during December to January, which lasts for three to four weeks. Gestation period is about 185 to 195 days. Musk Deer generally give birth to one, rarely two calves between April and June. Females fawn at selected places beneath dense shrubs, under low branches of fir, around fallen trees etc.

Threats to Survival

1. Poaching is undoubtedly the major threat to the survival of this species. Musk Deers were hunted for centuries and still being poached for the musk. Dried musk and musk pods are collected and are used extensively in the traditional Tibetan and Unani medicine in more than 400 preparations to cure heart and nervous disorders.
2. Musk has also been, used in the perfume industry.
3. Collection of one kilogram of musk requires the killing of 40 males. However, the poachers indiscriminately kill the specimens, irrespective of their sex and approximately 160 specimens are killed for 1 kg of musk.
4. Japan imported 250–300 kg musks annually from China. During 1857–58 Japan imported one lac sacs in a single year and during 1995–97, 1.5 tones of musk were exported from Russia to South Korea. This gives a fair idea about the threat that this species faces till date.

Conservation Measures

Although according to IUCN status, Musk Deer is designated as Lower Risk group and its local status is Uncommon, yet it is placed in the Schedule–I of Wildlife (Protection) Act, 1972, considering the degree of threats to its survival. Several protected areas have been declared within its distribution range. It has been included in the Appendix–I of CITES, thereby safeguarding this species from international trade. As a part of the *ex-situ* conservation of this species, captive populations are kept in Himachal Pradesh Musk Deer Farm (Kufri), Dachigram Sanctuary (Kashmir), Padmaja Naidu Himalayan Zoological Park (Darjeeling) and breeding enclosures at Kedarnath Wildlife Sanctuary. Breeding of Musk Deer and extraction of musk are done at Kufri. Sanctuaries and national parks on its distribution range protect its habitat. Introduction of synthetic products allied to musk has reduced demand of natural product to a great extent.

Prohibition of international trade by increasing vigilance on smuggling, encouraging the *in-situ* conservation, promoting education and research on this dwindling species and above all mass awareness campaign may be a few initiatives for better conservation of this species.

HIMALAYAN BROWN BEAR

Order: Carnivora

Family: Ursidae

***Ursus arctos isabellinus* (Horsfield)**

Common Name

Barf ka Reech, Safed Bhalu, Siala Reech, Lal Bhalu (Hindi); *Kane Haput (male), Kane Hapich (female)*(Kashmiri); *Drin mor* (Ladakhi); *Dub* (Nepali); *Red bear* (English)

Present Status

Wildlife (Protection) Act, 1972	Schedule–I
IUCN	Lower Risk
CITES	Appendix–I
Local Status	Rare

Distribution

Worldwide Distribution

It is found in the high altitudes of northwestern and central Himalayas and in Bhutan.

Distribution in India

In India, it is found in the high mountain ranges of Jammu and Kashmir, Himachal Pradesh, Uttaranchal and Sikkim. Their distribution varies from an altitude of 3000–6000 m.

Habitat

The bare open peaks situated much above the tree lines are the usual places for these bears. The Himalayan Brown Bear prefers alpine scrub and meadows and occasionally raids sub-alpine forests.

Distinctive Characters

Himalayan Brown Bear is a subspecies of Brown Bear and is comparatively smaller than the other subspecies. This is the largest bear species found in India and has a distinctive brown coat colour. This coat colour varies seasonally from light to dark. The white tips of their fur sometimes give the entire coat a silvery tinge. They lack the prominent chest marking which distinguishes them from the other bear species found in India.

Behavioural Biology

The Himalayan Brown Bear is terrestrial in nature and is least arboreal, which is a consequence of their adaptation to the undulating meadows in the alpine zone above tree line. It has a nocturnal mode of life. Mostly hibernate during winter inside cave, crevices of the rocks or inside a den dug out by them to pass the season buried deep under snow. Immediately after their 'winter sleep' they move to the higher reaches following the melting snowline. During late summer or early autumn, these bears migrate to the lower regions. Average life span of Himalayan Brown Bear is about 45–50 years.

Feeding Behaviour

The Himalayan Brown Bear is omnivorous in nature. During spring and in the early summer, once the ice is melted, the Himalayan Brown Bear graze in the alpine meadows on the newly grown grasses and engage themselves in upturning the stones in search of insects. They also feed on the hunting voles and marmots. During summer, they predate on sheep, goats, ponies and other livestocks which are engaged in grazing on alpine pastures. However, they avoid human beings. During late summer or early autumn, bears come down to lower reaches and feed on several wild fruits in the forests like berries, apricots, apples, mulberries, peaches and walnuts. They sometimes raid the orchards and the maize fields. They are also known to feed on the grass roots and tubers. When the food is scarce, they are also reported to feed on the carrion.

Reproductive Behaviour

Himalayan Brown Bears mate during early summer in May or June. Usually in December–January, the cubs are born in their winter retreat. The cubs stay with their mother till they are full grown and become independent. Once the cub is about 5–6 months old, they follow their mother in search of food.

Social Organization

Himalayan Brown Bears are generally solitary. There is no evidence of territorial defense and have overlapping home ranges. However, occasionally they may gather in large numbers at major food sources and family foraging groups are usually formed with dominance hierarchies. Highest-ranking individuals are large adult males and least aggressive and lowest-ranking are the adolescents. However, the most aggressive bears are females with youngs. The only social bonds formed are between females and youngs.

Threats to Survival

1. Poaching of the animals for hide, paw and gallbladder and bear bile. Some bear body parts (such as gall bladders) are used in Unani, Tibetan and similar other traditional medicinal practices for which the bears were often killed.
2. Himalayan Brown Bears have been widely sought for sport hunting as big game. They were also reported of being killed for their meat and hides. These animals are generally trapped using leg traps or noose traps laid in the trails frequently used by the bears.
3. Habitat disturbance throughout its distribution range due to human interference in the Indian range of its occurrence.
4. Human–Bear conflict occurs when the bears raid the crop fields for food (especially the ripe maize and sugarcane fields).

Conservation Measures

Himalayan Brown Bear is placed in the Schedule–I of Wildlife (Protection) Act, 1972, thus giving a countrywide legal protection. Though IUCN has categorized this species as Lower Risk, yet it is rarely seen throughout its distribution area. This species has also been placed under Appendix–I of CITES which altogether prohibits the trade of any part of these animals. In India, this animal is also protected in some of the conservation areas of Jammu & Kashmir and Himachal Pradesh and is best seen at the Great Himalayan National Park in Himachal Pradesh. Strict implementation of the Wildlife (Protection) Act is required and increased patrolling is necessary to protect these animals from being killed. Mass awareness among the locals in its distribution range and a conservation strategy through community participation could be a probable protection measure for the Himalayan Brown Bears.

LEOPARD

Order: Carnivora

Family: Felidae

***Panthera pardus* (Linnaeus)**

Common Name

Tendwa, Chita, Sona chita, Chita bagh (Hindi); *Karda, Asnea, Singhal, Bibalya wagh* (Marathi); *Chirchu, Chirate, Siwangi, Keeraba* (Kannar); *Chiruthai* (Tamil); *Chinna puli* (Telegu); *Thit* (Burmese); *Pulli poolee* (Malayalam); *Chita Bagh* (Bengali)

Present Status

Wildlife (Protection) Act, 1972	Schedule–I
IUCN	Lower Risk
CITES	Appendix–I
Local Status	Uncommon

Distribution

Worldwide Distribution

It occurs throughout the Asia, oriental region to Java and north to Korea, with the exception of high Tibetan plateau and Siberia and entire Africa except Sahara. It is also absent in Madagascar.

Distribution in India

Out of 14 subspecies of *Panthera pardus,* three subspecies are found in India namely *Panthera pardus fusca* (peninsular India, Sri Lanka), *Panthera pardus millardi* (Jammu and Kashmir) and *Panthera pardus pernigra* (Sikkim and Nepal). In India,

Leopard is found all over the country from the Himalayas to Cape Comorin, especially in the forests of plain lands and that of the mountains.

Habitat

Leopards can thrive in all kinds of habitat and are not restricted to the forests or dense vegetation cover. They can also dwell in the open country, grasslands and scrub forests as well as in the rocky surfaces.

Distinctive Characters

Leopard is much smaller than a tiger even when fully adult, being 170 to 215 cm in total length, including the tail and about 60 cm in shoulder height. Its coat is sleek and shorthaired. The ground colour is variable from pale yellow, warm gray, rich tawny to rufous fawn and has dark spots arranged in rosettes all over the sides of the body and the tail except at the tip, which is ringed. The spots, down the middle of the back and on the head, limbs and belly are solid black instead of being arranged in rosettes. Leopards have prominent whiskers. The forelimbs consist of 5 digits and the hind limbs consist of 4 digits with retractile claws.

The sexual dimorphism is very distinct in Leopard. The body size and the whiskers of the males are much bigger than the females. Males possess distinct scrotal sacs and conspicuous mammary gland is evident in the females, especially during the breeding seasons. The mammary gland is present along the ventro-lateral side of the body from the axilla to the groin.

Behavioural Biology

Leopards are semi arboreal and predatory in nature. They are generally nocturnal in habit. However, they frequently hunt by day, particularly if they fail to secure food at night. At daytime, they rest inside the bushes or on the tree branches with their tail and limbs hanging downwards. They are good climbers as well as efficient swimmers but are not very much fond of it.

In the forest, they prefer to follow the roads or paths or the beaten tracks of wild animals. It waits for its prey in the hiding and seizes the prey with either a sudden attack from the ground or by leaping on the prey from the height of an overhanging branch. They are generally solitary in nature and survive for seven to nine years in the wild.

Feeding Behaviour

Though medium sized, it may even kill animals larger than its own body size like cows, buffaloes etc. In forest, Leopards generally kill and eat anything it can overpower with safety such as cattle, deer, antelope, pig, hare, monkey, rodent and peafowl and quite a large number of birds. Leopards living near human settlements, particularly outside forest areas, prey mainly on domestic animals, calves, sheep and goats, on donkeys and quite commonly on the dogs. At times, due to non-availability of its natural food, few leopards turn into man-eaters and pose potential threat to human life. It has been reported that the amount of food consumed by a single leopard is 3.5–5 kg of meat daily.

Reproductive Behaviour

Leopards are polyestrous animals and are found to breed throughout the year. The estrous cycle lasts for 45 days. The females remain receptive for six to seven days at the middle of the estrous cycle. In nature the males follow the female in heat and there is severe competition among the males for mate selection. A receptive female shows different signs like restlessness, frequent micturation and occasional rolling on the ground. The sight of the heated female excites the male and soon it starts mating. The male copulates with the receptive female frequently but every time for a short duration. The gestation period lasts for roughly three months. One to three cubs are born at a time.

Social Organization

Leopards usually lead a solitary life. The males and the females associate during the breeding season. The female parent provides maximum parental care and the cubs suckle the breast of the mother up to 3 months of age. During this time the mother protects its cubs from all enemies and even from the other male Leopards. Leopards are territorial in nature and the territory of an individual is marked through spraying of urine on several stationary objects like tree trunks, rocks etc.

Threats to Survival

1. Destruction of the habitats of these animals is taking place due to extension of human settlements and agricultural lands, construction of roads and illegal logging.
2. Poaching of the animals for their hide and skin.
3. Human-Leopard conflict in several parts of the country.
4. Parasitic diseases are often found to kill a large number of these animals.
5. Periodic floods are also a cause of their dwindling population.

Conservation Measures

IUCN has listed this species as Lower Risk considering its global population status. However, considering its present threats, it is placed in the Schedule–I of Wildlife (Protection) Act, 1972, providing the animal a nationwide legal protection. Several protected areas have been declared within its habitat to protect this species as well as to safeguard its habitat. Leopard was once the most abundant among the large cats in India and Pakistan, but their populations have been greatly reduced through excessive hunting for skin trade and loss of habitat due to agricultural development. In India, there is a complete ban on export of of wild pelts since 1979. The International Fur Trade Federation has also imposed ban on the use of leopard skins and the animal was also incorporated in the Appendix–I of CITES, thereby preventing any of its part from being traded.

Conservation Measures: Indian Initiatives

Despite an exploding population of humans, India is still rich in biodiversity which ranges from large number of charismatic megafauna to microorganisms including a variety of aquatic and terrestrial flora. It is indeed a treasure house of biological diversity as well as an important center of endemism having a large number and variety of endemic flora and fauna. It is presently one of the few megadiversity countries of the world, incorporating three biodiversity hotspots within its geographical boundaries. India presently harbours about 60 percent of global Tiger population, 50 percent of Asian Elephant and 80 percent of Greater One-horned Rhinoceros. In spite of being rich in wildlife and biodiversity, threat of extinction looms large on several species. Habitat destruction has been undoubtedly one of the biggest threats to a large number of species over the globe and till date it is the most difficult one to mitigate. In the past few decades, world consumption of wood has increased by 22 percent globally and paper usage has increased by 41 percent. In many parts of the globe, forests are being converted to productive farmlands. It is estimated that only about 30 percent of Africa's original moist forests remain at present. In addition to this, pollution of air and water also threaten the survival of many wild species. Pesticides, chemical run-offs, industrial wastes kill many species present in the soil and aquatic ecosystems. Marine oil slicks cause serious mortalities of several marine species including sea mammals and birds. Pollution by the gases produced by industries are often trapped in the atmosphere and lead to even greater problems like ozone layer depletion, green house effect, ultimately leading to global warming and climate change. In addition to this, much of the depletion of wildlife in the recent past can be attributed to over-exploitation of the ecosystems and natural resources in order to quench the 'need and greed' of ever increasing human population. While habitat loss poses the most serious and long-term threat to the survival of wildlife, hunting, unsustainable use and commercial exploitation of wildlife are other exterminating factors associated with human greed.

The history of utilization of natural and biological resources by man throughout the globe dates back to prehistoric times when man hunted wild species for food and other basic prerequisites for his survival. In the process of civilization and evolution, few millenniums later, the *Homo sapiens* learnt to use tools and discovered wheel, fire and started to grow food grains. Before human adopted agricultural practices, they were solely dependent on the wild fauna and flora to meet the basic needs for their survival like food, clothing and shelter. As time passed, traditional hunting had been joined by commercial hunting to supply large, settled, agrarian based populations with consumer goods. Subsequently, wild flora and fauna continued to cater to the essential needs as well as to the amusement and fashion of the consumers of the distant lands. As a result, a few centuries before the Christ, an international trade in wild flora and fauna came into being. Moreover, since local medicinal practices became trans-regional, plant and animal derivatives formed a major part of this international trade. Later, the industrial revolution led to an increased demand for these bioresources and also made their transportation easier. Thus a paradigm shift occurred in the trade modalities and the supply was thought to be inexhaustible, which was not actually so. As a consequence, several species became extinct or at least locally extinct, due to over-harvesting for either local use or trade. Still at that time the alarm was not raised. Roughly during the middle of the 20th century, serious conservation efforts were initiated and it was realized that the combined effect of destruction and subsequent shrinkage of habitat and the trade has threatened the existence of a large number of species.

Indian culture shows a tradition of love, respect and reverence for all life forms and is based on an ardent faith of conservation which was reflected in the daily lives of the people as well as in the ancient myths, folklores, literatures and traditional rituals. Several monks, saints and religious leaders asked common people to be more compassionate for all living creatures around them. Through religion or ancient folklores, the message of conservation was spread among the common people and as a consequence, admiration for wildlife became a part of their lifestyle and culture. Pioneering effort was made by Emperor Ashoka, who formulated one of the earliest conservation laws during the third century B.C. He defined a king's duty as not only to protect the citizens and maintain law and order, but also to preserve animal life and forests as well. In the later part of his reign, Ashoka brought about significant changes in his style of governance. Embracing Buddhism, he protected many birds and animals and even imposed ban on the royal hunt and introduced a fine of 100 *panas* or coins for poaching deers inside the forests. *Ahimsa* (non-violence) indeed became the central concept of the religious belief of Buddhism and Jainism in the 7th and 6th centuries B.C. Jain religious beliefs even speak to avoid harming the worms and insects. These ideas later formed a part of the Hindu religion and were passed through centuries that followed.

The Hindu religion has many deities with animal attributes that reflect the relation between man and nature in India. In addition to these, several living representatives of animal species are also honoured. According to legends, the monkey god *Hanuman* was the chief of a troop of monkeys. In the epic, *Ramayana,* he was portrayed as a selfless hero who had assisted lord Rama to recover his wife from demon Ravana. The elephant-headed *Ganesha* is worshipped as the god of wisdom and prosperity. Shiva's bull mount, *Nandi,* is not a god but plays an important accessory role, as it is believed that through him Shiva may be asked for help and support. Several other animal figures in Hindu tradition are being associated with various gods as vehicles or through some other beliefs. The peacock is associated with *Kartikeya, Skandha* and lord *Krishna.* The winged *Garuda,* with the beak and talons of an eagle and the body of a man carries *Vishnu.* Rat is the mount of *Ganesha.* Buffalo demon *Mahisha* is celebrated during the festival of *Durgapuja* in Bengal. The mount of Lord *Brahma* and *Saraswati* are *Hansa,* the wild goose. There are also several animal incarnations or *avatars* of *Vishnu* that were believed to save mankind from several calamities. Being associated with the deities has safeguarded several wild species from perishing in the hands of the humans through ages.

Several tribal rituals in our country also reflect the age old respect for wild flora and fauna. The Warli tribe in the north of Mumbai worships *Vaghadeva,* the tiger god. Tigers are worshipped in several other parts of the country as well. In Sunderbans, the forest dwellers as well as the people entering inside the forest worship *Banabibi* and *Dakshinray,* who are believed to be the lord of the mangrove forests and will protect them from all evils inside the forests. The Bishnois are cast of farmers in Rajasthan who adhere to "twenty-nine" commandments as laid down in their holy scripture, four of which refer especially to the protection of wildlife and natural resources. They believe that the spirits of their ancestors reside in the blackbucks. This simple belief motivates them to protect the herds of blackbuck and chinkara grazing on their land from the hunters and poachers. Their houses are mostly made up of local natural materials and they follow a strict conservation of timber resources by collecting only dead wood for fuel. The Khezri trees are worshipped by the Bishnois. In 1730, the soldiers of the then *maharaja* tried to cut the *Khezri* trees in a Bishnoi village which was noticed by one Bishnoi woman, Amrita Devi. She, her children and the fellow villagers embraced the trees to protect them. In the ensuing slaughter, 362 villagers died. This incidence of sacrifice was the inspiration of the modern Chipko movement. Even more fascinating are the local beliefs in many parts of India against killing of certain species or when they may not be put to death. The tribals of Thane rarely harmed wild dogs while the Kolis valued the packs of these carnivores for curbing the number of deers and chasing away tigers that might lift their valuable cattle. The Baghel Rajputs in central India never take part in the pursuit of the tigers as they claim to be the descendents of these big cats. Sloth bears are believed to be the descendants of *Jambovan,* a bear hero in Ramayana, which safeguard this species in many parts of India. In the past, peacocks were supposed to save crop field from snakes and insect pests and was, therefore, guarded from hunters. Even the creatures that were potentially dangerous were not always killed. Co-existence was a part of human lifestyle. In the rural India, still today, there are several land areas, hedges and forest patches where cutting a tree or killing any life form is forbidden by religion or access to common people is restricted. These areas, known as 'sacred groves', serve as last refuge for several species of flora and fauna. There are evidences that several forest tribes worship certain parts of the forests and almost in every village, there are several old trees, which are worshipped as 'sacred tree'. These patches when given a closer look are found to be teeming with rich diversity of life. Though, sacredness or taboos are not universal, yet, these norms undoubtedly played a crucial role in the survival of the thriving populations of certain plants and animals atleast at certain places. Perhaps the low density of human population and large areas of forest and fallow limited conflict in the past. The Chinese traveller, Hiuen Tsang, in his travel across the India during 17th century A.D. repeatedly refers to the dense forests tracts that made his journey difficult. The ecological map of the entire south Asia was indeed strikingly different from the one we know today. It was mostly covered by the forests with fewer cultivated lands in between. Obviously, the fear of natural forces was also another reason which led to the worshipping of several natural entities, be it the association of several animals with divinity or the worship of fire and water.

Before colonialism, the Mughal states honoured the local customs and were very much conscious about harming local sentiments. However, during this period hunting was an essential practice related to warfare. During winter, the ruler used to hunt with thousands of his soldiers in a patch of jungle. All animals caught were considered as ruler's prey–a part of which was often sold and few were also distributed among the poor. Rulers used to declare few areas of the forests as 'reserved' where intrusion of common people was restricted. These areas supplied many valuable animals, like cheetahs for hunting, elephants for warfare etc.

Under the British, things changed radically and at one level several ideological and commercial reasons let to the uncontrolled killing of several wild flora and fauna. British thought to exterminate the carnivores as they were treated as vermins. Subsequently, the hunting of wild beasts became a *sports-per-excellence* which was believed to symbolize the hyper masculinity of the British colonial power. Gradually, *shikar* replaced *ahimsa* and became a part of the culture and festive occasions of the elites. Several game associations were formed to regulate 'game hunting' by introducing several norms, rules and modes of hunting. This indiscriminate killing of animals associated with reclamation of forests for revenue lands, led to sharp decline in the number of several wild species. Worried by this sharp decline in animal population and to maintain hunting as an imperial sport, officials realized the need for animal conservation for their own interest and thus a new regime for conservation of wildlife arose. Forest laws were introduced to protect forests from grazing, trapping and gleaning and to establish their control over commercially valuable timber and other forest produces. Thus, colonial forest laws and game laws were introduced actually to exclude the locals from being a part of the conservation processes.

In the post independence era, Pandit Jawaharlal Nehru, the first Prime Minister of India, immediately initiated measures to protect Indian wildlife. As a consequence, the Indian Board of Wildlife (IBWL) was formed in 1952. But it took time for this new domain of conservation to be properly established. Through the 1950s and 1960s, the princes still continued with their *shikars* further depleting several wild species. In addition to this, wide expansion of agriculture considerably reduced the forest cover and booming markets encouraged large-scale exports of animals and hides. These pressures had led a lot many species to the verge of extinction, if they had still not ceased to survive. Over 70,000 monkeys were exported in 1951 and 1952 alone. Leopards and tigers were poisoned with pesticides and monkeys and macaques were exported to the west to earn foreign currencies. Mrs. Indira Gandhi, who addressed a major international conference in New Delhi in 1969, eventually put this gloomy situation to an end. The 1970s saw the beginning of a new and more resolute initiative towards conservation. The export of several wildlife articles including tiger and leopard skins were banned, a new act with stronger punitive powers and a long list of protected species was brought into force in the name of Wildlife (Protection) Act in the year 1972. Project Tiger was launched in 1973 that not only sought to protect the species, but also was provided with federal funding for the establishment of nine reserves in different habitats. Project Tiger was followed by several other species-specific conservation projects. A new era of wildlife conservation began.

Legal Perspectives of Wildlife Conservation

In India, several legislative measures have been adopted for the protection of wildlife in the country.

1. Directive Principles and State Policy

The need of wildlife conservation has been incorporated in the Indian constitution. In Article 48–A of Directive Principles of State Policy, the following duties for the state and the citizens are laid down:

> *"The state shall endeavor to protect and improve the environment and to safeguard the forests and wildlife of the country".*

Article 51–A interalia states that:

> *"It shall be the duty of every citizen of India to protect and improve the natural environment including forests, lakes, rivers and wildlife and to have passion for living creatures."*

The 42nd Amendment of constitution in 1976 has incorporated forest and wildlife in the concurrent list which means besides controlling the protection and preservation of wildlife, central government can acquire certain forests and wildlife sanctuaries of national importance under the powers of acquisition of property [Entry 42 of Union list]. The 73rd Amendment of constitution in 1992 has to some extent linked the panchayats to environment protection and conservation.

2. National Acts Related to Wildlife Conservation

The state and central authorities have made several acts from time to time to protect wildlife and check their decline. Some important acts are:

1. Madras Wild Elephant Preservation Act, 1873
2. All India Elephant Preservation Act, 1879

3. Wild Birds and Animals Preservation Act, 1912
4. Bengal Rhinoceros Preservation Act, 1932
5. Bombay Wild Animals and Wild Birds Protection Act, 1951
6. Assam Rhinoceros Protection Act, 1954
7. Indian Wildlife (Protection) Act, 1972
8. Forest Protection Act, 1980
9. The Biological Diversity Act, 2002

Indian Wildlife (Protection) Act, 1972

Based on the recommendations of the Indian Board of Wildlife (IBWL), the Wildlife (Protection) Act (WPA) was passed by the parliament in 1972. This act was adopted by all the states except Jammu and Kashmir, which has their own state act. Wildlife (Protection) Act provides legal protection to wildlife in general and threatened species in particular. It has provisions of setting up of national parks and sanctuaries where the wild species can receive greater protection (Chapter IV of WPA). Wildlife (Protection) Act, 1972 has several chapters dealing with:

> Authorities to be appointed; Hunting of wild animals; Protection of specified plants; Protected Areas; Central Zoo Authority and recognition of Zoos; Regulation of trade or commerce in wild animals, Animal articles and trophies; Prevention and detection of offences etc. Wild animals are enlisted in five different 'Schedules' specified in the WPA.

Schedule I: Includes rare and threatened animals

Schedule II: Includes animals that enjoy special game status

Schedule III: Includes big games (wild animals)

Schedule IV: Includes small games (wild animals)

Schedule V: Includes vermins (wild animals)

Some of the highlighting features of Wildlife (Protection) Act, 1972 are depicted below :

The animals listed in these schedules are provided with stringent protection under legislation, hunting is banned and strict control measures are imposed on it.

Section 9 of the act prohibits hunting of any wild animals specified in Schedule I, II, III and IV. There are also stricter provisions and procedures to deal with regarding the stocks of wildlife articles held by the dealers, transportation of wildlife and deterrent punishment to the poachers.

Article 35 clause 6 of the WPA, 1972 states that no person shall destroy, exploit or remove any wild animal or deprive any wild animal of its habitat within such national parks except under and in accordance with permit granted by the Chief

Wildlife Warden and no such permit shall be granted unless the state government, being satisfied that such destruction, exploitation or removal of wildlife from the national park is necessary for the improvement and better management of wildlife therein, authorizes the issue of such permit.

According to the **Section 49A of the WPA, 1972,** "scheduled animal" means an animal specified for the time being in Schedule I or Part II of Schedule II and "scheduled animal article" means an article made from any scheduled animal and includes an article or object in which the whole or any part of such animal has been used [However, it does not include tail feather of peacock, an article or trophy made there from and snake venom or its derivative].

According to the **Section 61 of the WPA, 1972,** the central government may, if it is of opinion that it is expedient so to do, by notification, add or delete any entry to or from any Schedule or transfer any entry from one Part of a Schedule to another Part of the same Schedule or from one Schedule to another. On the issue of a notification, the relevant Schedule shall be deemed to be altered accordingly, provided that every such alteration shall be without prejudice to anything done or omitted to be done before such alteration.

According to the **Section 62 of the WPA, 1972,** the central government may, by notification, declare any wild animal, other than those specified in Schedule I and Part II of Schedule II, to be vermin for any area and for such period as may be specified therein and so long as such notification is in force, such wild animal shall be deemed to have been included in Schedule V.

Biological Diversity Act, 2002

India is a signatory to the Convention on Biological Diversity (CBD) since February 1994 and is one of the first few countries to have enacted an appropriate comprehensive legislation to achieve the objectives of the convention. As signatory to the CBD. India has met three positive obligations *viz.* (i) *Submission of a status report*–A report entitled "Status of Biodiversity in India, was prepared in 1997 and submitted in 1998; (ii) *Submission of National Biodiversity Strategy and Action Plan (NBSAP)*–The report was prepared over a period of three years and submitted in October, 2002 and (iii) *Enacting laws to protect biodiversity of the country*–The Biological Diversity Act, 2002, passed on December 11, 2002 came into force on February 5, 2003, followed by the formation of the Biological Diversity Rules, 2004. The Biological Diversity Act of 2002 provides necessary statutory and administrative mechanism at the national level to realize the objectives of CBD. The main intent of the legislation is to protect India's rich biodiversity and associated knowledge against their use by foreign individuals and organizations without sharing the benefits arising out of such use and to check bio-piracy.

The Biological Diversity Act, 2002 is an Act to provide for conservation of biological diversity, sustainable use of its components and fair and equitable sharing of the benefits arising out of the use of biological resources, knowledge and for matters connected therewith or incidental thereto.

Regulation of Access to Biological Diversity

1. Certain persons not to undertake biodiversity related activities without approval of National Biodiversity Authority (Section 3).
2. Results of research not to be transferred to certain persons without approval of National Biodiversity Authority except certain collaborative research projects (Section 4).

   Certain person in the above two sections refers to:

   (a) *a person who is not a citizen of India;*

   (b) *a citizen of India, who is a non-resident as defined I clause (30) of section 2 of the Income Tax Act, 1961;*

   (c) *a body corporate, association or organization:*

   (i) *not incorporated or registered in India; or*

   (ii) *incorporated or registered in India under any law for the time being in force which has any non-Indian participation in its share capital or management.*
3. Application for intellectual property rights not to be made without approval of National Biodiversity Authority (Section 6).
4. Prior intimation to State Biodiversity Board for obtaining biological resource for certain purposes (Section 7).

   No person, who is a citizen of India or a body corporate, association or organization, which is registered in India, shall obtain any biological resource for the **purpose of commercial utilization, or bio-survey and bio-utilization for commercial utilization** except after giving prior intimation to the State Biodiversity Board concerned;

   Provided that the provisions of this section shall not apply to the local people and communities of the area, including growers and cultivators of biodiversity, and vaids and hakims, who have been practicing indigenous medicines.

Source: The Biological Diversity Act, 2002

3. Convention on International Trade in Endangered Species of Wild Fauna and Flora (CITES)

The Convention on International Trade in Endangered Species of Wild Fauna and Flora (CITES) came into effect in the year 1975. As the name suggests, this convention aims to prevent and/or regulate international trade in different parts of endangered species. India is a signatory to this convention. This convention controls the trade of all the species listed in its 'Appendix'. There are three Appendices and the Appendices I, II and III to the Convention are lists of species which are afforded with different levels or types of protection from over-exploitation. The countries which are signatory to this convention are referred to as the 'Parties' and these parties cannot import or export the species that is listed under the CITES without proper licenses. Species may be added to or removed from Appendices–I and II, or moved between them, only by the Conference of the Parties, either at its regular meetings or by postal procedures. But species may be added to or removed from Appendix III at any time and by any Party unilaterally (although the Conference of the Parties has recommended that changes be timed to coincide with amendments to Appendices–I and II).

Appendix I contains species that are most endangered among CITES-listed animals and plants and are threatened with extinction. CITES generally prohibits commercial international trade in specimens of these species, however, trade may be allowed under exceptional circumstances, *e.g.* for scientific research. In these cases, trade may be authorized by the granting of both an export permit (or re-export certificate) and an import permit. (Article III of the Convention)

Appendix II contains species that are not necessarily threatened with extinction at present but that may become so unless trade is closely controlled. It also includes so-called "look-alike species", *i.e.* species of which the specimens in trade look like those of species listed for conservation reasons (Article II, paragraph 2 of the Convention). International trade in Appendix–II species may be authorized by the granting of an export permit or re-export certificate. No import permit is necessary for these species under CITES (although a permit is needed in some countries that have taken stricter measures than CITES requires). Permits or certificates should only be granted if the relevant authorities are satisfied that certain conditions are met, above all that trade will not be detrimental to the survival of the species in the wild. (Article IV of the Convention)

Appendix III is a list of species included at the request of a Party that already regulates trade in the species and that needs the cooperation of other countries to prevent unsustainable or illegal exploitation (Article II, paragraph 3, of the Convention). International trade in species listed in this Appendix is allowed only on presentation of the appropriate permits or certificates. (Article V of the Convention)

Source: http://www.cites.org/eng/app/index.shtml

In each country, there are specific administrative setups to implement the provisions of the Convention. In India, Inspector General of Forests and the Director of Wildlife Preservation, Government of India, have been designated as the management authorities of the CITES. The Director, Zoological Survey of India; the Director, Botanical Survey of India and the Director, Central Marine Research Institute are the authorities for the scientific and technical inputs. To regulate the international trade four ports *viz.* Mumbai, Delhi, Kolkata and Chennai are controlled by the Wildlife

Preservation Wing and is supervised by the Deputy Directors posted at these places for supervising the trade (*viz.* Deputy Director–Northern Region, Deputy Director–Southern Region, Deputy Director–Eastern Region and Deputy Director–Western Region). CITES is a major step for regulating the wildlife trade as because it provides cooperation at the international level without which illegal trade could not be controlled.

Parallel to CITES, another Convention on Migratory Birds have also been signed between India and Russia with an objective to protect the trans-boundary migratory birds which annually migrate during winter from these trans-Himalayan regions to India.

Conservation through National/State Animals and Plants

An alternative and effective way of conserving indigenous wildlife is to assign them a status quo. Accordingly, each state has declared one mammal, bird, tree and flower as their state mammal, state bird, state tree and state flower, which in turn, ensure protection of these species in the state. Subsequently, based on nativity, endemism, general importance and several other criteria, a list of 108 species (27 each of mammals, birds, trees and flowers) has been prepared with the help of Zoological Survey of India, Botanical Survey of India, National Botanical Research Institute and National Bureau of Plant Genetic Resources. It is the states responsibility to take up necessary legislative procedures to declare them, to ensure their conservation and to take necessary steps to increase their population size especially in the relevant conservation areas within the state.

State/ Union Territories	*Animal (Mammal)*	*Bird*	*Tree*	*Flower*
Andhra Prdaesh	Blackbuck	Indian Roller	Neem	*
Arunachal Pradesh	Mithun	Great Hornbill	Hollong	Lady slipper Orchid
Assam	*	*	*	*
Bihar	Gaur	Indian Roller	Peepal	Kachnar
Chhattisgarh	Wild Buffalo	Hill Myna	*	*
Delhi	*	*	*	*
Goa	Gaur	Black Crested Bulbul	Asna	*
Gujarat	Asiatic Lion	Greater Flamingo	*	*
Haryana	Blackbuck	Black Francolin	Peepal	Lotus
Himachal Pradesh	Musk Deer	Monal	Deodar	Rhododendron
Jammu and Kashmir	Hangul	Black-necked Crane	Chinar	Lotus
Jharkhand	Elephant	Koel	Sal	Palash
Karnataka	Elephant	Indian Roller	Sandal	Lotus
Kerala	Elephant	Great Hornbill	Coconut	Kanikonna

Contd...

State/ Union Territories	Animal (Mammal)	Bird	Tree	Flower
Madhya Pradesh	Swamp Deer	Paradise Fly Catcher	*	*
Maharashtra	Indian Giant Squirrel	Green Imperial Pigeon	Mango	Jarul
Manipur	Sangai	Mrs. Hume's Pheasant	Toon	Shirhoy Lilly
Meghalaya	Clouded Leopard	Hill Myna	Gamari	Lady slipper Orchid
Mizoram	Hoolock Gibbon	Mrs. Hume's Pheasant	Iron Wood	Red Vanda
Nagaland	Mithun	Blyth's Tragopan	Alder	Rhododendron
Orissa	Elephant	Peacock	Banyan	Lotus
Punjab	Blackbuck	Northern Goshawk	Sheesham	*
Rajasthan	Chinkara	Great Indian Bustard	Khejri	Rohira
Sikkim	Red Panda	Blood Pheasant	Rhododendron	Nobile Orchid
Tamil Nadu	Nilgir Tahr	Emerald Dove	Palmera Palm	Kandhal
Tripura	Phayre's langur	Green Imperial Pigeon	Agar	Nageshwar
Uttaranchal	Himalayan Musk Deer	Himalayan Monal	Burans	Brahm Kamal
Uttar Pradesh	Swamp Deer	Sarus Crane	Ashok	Brahm Kamal
West Bengal	Fishing Cat	White-throated Kingfisher	Chatian	Shephali
Andaman and Nicober Islands	*	*	*	*
Chandigarh	*	*	*	*
Dadar and Nagar Haveli	*	*	*	*
Daman and Diu	*	*	*	*
Lakshdweep	Butterfly Fish	Sooty Tern	Bread Fruit	*
Pondicherry	*	*	*	*

* To be declared.

Source: Sinha, 2001.

Moreover, the Government of India has declared Tiger [*Panthera tigris*] as national animal, Indian Peafowl [*Pavo christatus*] as national bird, Banyan [*Ficus benghalensis*] as national tree, Lotus [*Nelumbo nucifera*] as national flower and Mango [*Mangifera indica*] as the national fruit of India

Special Conservation Projects

To protect the endangered flora and fauna of our country, the government, non-government organizations, different institutes and universities have initiated several special conservation projects. Most of these projects are either funded by the Ministry of Environment and Forests, several government departments or has been taken up by several non-governmental organizations. Few of these projects are also funded by several foreign organizations and multinational corporates as well. Few of these noteworthy conservation projects are:-

Save the Barasingha Campaign

In 1969, Government of Madhya Pradesh launched this campaign and was supported by the Government of India. The *Barasingha* or Swamp Deer [*Cervus duvaucelii*] was once plentiful in the north, central and eastern India. But this species had undergone a sharp population decline and a census in and around Kanha in 1970 recorded only 66 individuals in that area (Khajuria and Sinha, 1986; Caughley and Gunn, 1996). Immediately several action plan was adopted to save the animal from becoming extinct which involved removal of human population from the area, regeneration of grasslands, habitat improvement and reclamation of habitat as well as construction of enclosures and strict anti-poaching measures. As a consequence of these strict conservation initiatives, the number of swamp deer increased from 66 in 1970 to 574 in 1988. Presently the total population of three subspecies [*Cervus duvaucelii branderi, Cervus duvaucelii duvaucelii, Cervus duvaucelii ranjitsinhi*] in India is around 3200 individuals (Nowak, 1999).

Cervus duvaucelii branderi

§ 1938: 3000 (Caughley and Gunn, 1996)
§ 1970: 66 (Caughley and Gunn, 1996)
§ 1977: 283 (Caughley and Gunn, 1996)
§ 1999: 400 (Nowak, 1999)

Cervus duvaucelii duvaucelii

§ 1972: 1320 (Dudhwa National Park, India) (Nowak, 1999)
§ 1989: 765 (Dudhwa National Park, India) (Nowak, 1999)
§ 1999: 2000 (Nepal) (Nowak, 1999)

Cervus duvaucelii ranjitsinhi

§ 1999: 800 (Kaziranga National Park, Assam, India) (Nowak, 1999)

Gir Lion Sanctuary Project

The The factors that threatened the very existence of the Asiatic Lions include unabated shooting, reduction of natural habitat due to rapid increase of agriculture, water pollution by the local villagers and drastic reduction of their natural prey base of wild ungulate population, which subsequently gave rise in increased cattle killing by the lions and greater amount of Human–Lion conflict. The Gir Lion Sanctuary project was initiated in 1972, with one of its main objectives being to remove the local indigenous people (Maldharis) from the interior of the park. The reason for the displacement of this devoutly religious pastoral community was their on-going conflict with the Gir Lions. In the distant past, plenty of water and grazing was available in Gir and the Maldharis and the magnificent Asiatic Lions co-existed with little conflict. Lions were not interested in domestic livestock and the Maldharis were able to protect their stock with relative ease. Prior to and after independence, conditions in Gir deteriorated rapidly and affected both of the Maldharis and the lions. Widespread destruction of private forests was initiated when the owners got wind of the likely takeover of their forests by the newly formed state government. This was followed by hydro-electric projects, which involved the mass clearance of forests, for example the Ukai project in south Gujarat which involved the sacrifice of 40,000 hectares of teak forest. Habitat loss, as with all the parks in India, is usually the catalyst for conflict between local people and the resident wildlife. Good quality grazing became scarcer and financial inducements were offered to the Maldharis to allow illegal entry of large number of cattles, many of which came from areas far from the park. This huge increase in cattles was a bonanza for the lion prides who were losing a lot of their prey species such as chital and sambar due to habitat destruction.

A five year plan was proposed by the government of Gujarat to protect the Asiatic Lions [*Panthera leo persica*] inside the Gir forests. All these factors were considered and mitigated in a best possible way under this project to ensure the survival of Asiatic Lions in their last refuge inside 1515 sq km forest of Kathiawar district, later designated as Gir Sanctuary. As a consequence, the lion population has increased from 177 in 1968 to 180 in 1984. At present, a core area of 258.7 sq km is declared as National Park and the ecological balance of the park is properly maintained. With these recent efforts, the number of Asiatic Lions has increased and at present there are about 300 lions inside the park. The park is one of the best protected sanctuaries in India with as many as eight hundred guards patrolling the entire park. The lions' prey species have increased in number under the protection of the park authorities. The lions' feeding habits have changed back to a 'normal' pattern with wild ungulates accounting for seventy percent of their kills. Thus Gir Lion Sanctuary is definitely one of the India's success stories.

Project Tiger

Project Tiger was launched in the year 1973. Initially, during the period 1973–74, nine tiger reserves were established in different states by the central and state governments. These nine reserves covered an area of about 13,017sq km. *viz.* Manas (Assam), Palamau (Bihar), Similipal (Orissa), Corbett (U.P.), Kanha (M.P.), Melghat (Maharashtra), Bandipur (Karnataka), Ranthambhore (Rajasthan) and Sunderbans (West Bengal). All these tiger reserves were created in the country on a 'core-buffer' strategy. A minimum core of 300 sq km with a sizeable buffer was recommended for each project area. The project started as a 'Central Sector Scheme' with the full assistance of central government till 1979–80. Later, it became a 'Centrally Sponsored Scheme' from 1980–81, with equal sharing of expenditure between the centre and the states. The W.W.F. has given an assistance of US $ one million in the form of equipments, expertise and literature.

The core areas were fred from all sorts of human activities and the buffer areas were subjected to 'conservation oriented land use'. The overall administration of the project is monitored by a 'Steering Committee'. For the proper execution of the project the respective state governments appointed a 'Field Director' for each reserve, who is assisted by the field and technical personnel. The Chief Wildlife Wardens in various states are responsible for the field execution. A full-fledged 'Director' of the project centrally coordinates the work for the country.

Main objectives of Project Tiger include:

1. Identify the limiting factors and to mitigate them by suitable management.
2. Elimination of all forms of human exploitations and biotic disturbances from the core area and rationalization of activities in the buffer zone.
3. Restricting the habitat management only to repair the damages done to the eco-system by human and other interferences, so as to facilitate recovery of the eco-system to its natural state.
4. Monitoring the faunal and floral changes over time and carrying out research about wildlife.
5. Management practices, which tend to push the wildlife populations beyond the carrying capacity of the habitat, were carefully avoided.

Project Tiger is one of the successful conservation projects in India and through the 'restorative management' and 'intense protection' under 'Project Tiger' have saved many of our eco-typical areas from destruction and the tiger population in the reserve areas have increased from a mere 268 in 9 reserves in 1972 to 1576 in 27 reserves in 2003. The main achievements of this project are fire protection through suitable preventive and control measures and habitat recovery. In the subsequent 'Five Year Plans', the main thrust was to enlarge the core and buffer zones in certain reserves, intensification of protection and eco-development in the buffer zones of existing tiger reserves, creation of additional tiger reserves and strengthening of the research activities. Wireless communication system and outstation patrol camps have also been developed within the tiger reserves to deter the poachers away from these reserves. Voluntary village realocation has been done in many reserves, especially from the core area. In Kanha, Bandipur and Ranthambhore, all the villages have been shifted from the core and after realocation, the villagers have been provided with alternate agricultural lands and other community benefits. The area around the buffer is now contemplated as a zone of multiple uses by the neighbouring communities, to bring compatibility between the reserves and the local community and to involve the locals in tiger conservation.

A viable tiger population in a habitat indicates the presence of a good prey base, which in turn will depend on undisturbed forest vegetation. Tiger, being at the apex of the food chain, can be considered as the indicator of the stability of the entire ecosystem. Thus, 'Project Tiger', is basically the conservation of the entire ecosystem and apart from tigers, all other wild animals also have increased in number in the project areas. Since thousands of indigenous communities depend on tiger habitats, we cannot view these protected areas in isolation from the surrounding socioeconomic realities and developmental priorities of the government. This calls for a cross-sectoral and cross-disciplinary approach. Regional planning and active community participation around tiger reserves with integrated land-use planning is of utmost importance in our country for effective tiger conservation.

Source: http://projecttiger.nic.in

Operation Rhino

The Greater One-horned Rhinoceros (*Rhinoceros unicornis* Linnaeus) is known to have once been extremely common and widespread in the Indo-Gengetic plains of the north, central and south-eastern parts of the country. By the end of the 17th century, it had completely disappeared from much of the range and presently is confined, as small populations, in few protected areas in India, in habitats comprised of riparian grasslands, shallow and dense woodlands. The fragmentation of habitats by human activities, however, often prevents migrations and genetic exchange among populations. As a consequence, local population become isolated and cause "inbreeding". Nevertheless, a primary goal of conservation efforts has been to preserve a maximum amount of genetic variation in each species.

Anti-poaching measures have been intensified by regular patrolling, constitution of special protection force, strengthening communication networks, provision of better arms for staff, coordination of law enforcement agencies, incentives and rewards, publicity/nature education/awareness generation and eco-development activities for fringe villages. Habitat improvement works are done by canopy manipulation in woodlands, planting of indigenous fodder grasses, weed eradication, control burning and fire control, grazing control of domestic livestock and flood embankment protection works and soil moisture conservation works.

The Wildlife Wing of the Govt. of West Bengal in collaboration with the Wildlife Institute of India, Dehradun and the National Institute of Immunology, New Delhi, therefore, undertook a study for genetic fingerprinting of rhino population distributed within this state. In order to gain an insight into the organizational aspects of the genome, a study on the DNA sequence variability within and between the rhino species was undertaken. It is envisaged that a detailed understanding on genetic variability would greatly facilitate the effective conservation of this species. The resultant information would also enable to compare Rhino genomes from two designated protected areas (*viz.* Gorumara National Park and Jaldapara Wildlife Sanctuary) and later even from other parts of the world. The purpose of the present study was to establish the pattern and extent of genetic variation at the DNA sequence level among the rhino population in West Bengal using conventional DNA profiling and other biotechnological approaches. Further, it was aimed to develop species specific DNA probe so that the same may be used for ascertaining the origin of tissues, bone or horn samples in forensic or poaching cases.

Source: http://education.vsnl.com/bengaltiger/

Project Elephant

Project Elephant was launched in the year 1991–92 with an objective to ensure long-term survival of the viable population of elephants in their natural habitats.

States having populations of wild elephants are being given financial support as well as technical and scientific assistance to fulfil the objectives of this project and ultimately to conserve Asian Elephants in their natural habitats. An amount of Rs. 3.05 crore (approx) was allocated to the elephant range states to enable them to provide financial assistance for habitat management, to mitigate man-elephant conflict, payment of ex-gratia relief for loss of life and properties, strengthening of anti-poaching measures, capture and translocation of problematic elephant populations etc. Further, an amount of Rs. 142.30 lakh was released to the elephant range states to strengthen their anti-poaching and anti-depredation activities. Main activities of Project Elephant include:

1. Ecological restoration of existing natural habitats and migratory routes (corridors) of elephants.
2. Development of scientific management plan for conservation of elephant habitats.
3. Scientific planning to ensure survival of a viable population of wild Asiatic Elephants in India.
4. Promote measures for mitigation of man-elephant conflict in general, especially in crucial habitats.
5. Development of strategies to minimize pressures of human and domestic stock activities in crucial elephant habitats.
6. Strengthening of anti-poaching activities and patrolling for protection of wild elephants form poachers and unnatural causes of death.
7. Research on issues related to management and *in-situ* conservation of Asiatic Elephant.
8. Awareness generation programme through mass education and a series of workshops, seminars, meetings etc.
9. Eco-development projects to involve the local people in the conservation action programme.
10. Veterinary care.

Source: http://www.envfor.nic.in/pe/pe.html

Snow Leopard Breeding Project

In India, where Snow Leopards occur on the southern slopes of the Himalayas, the species is under full protection since 1952. Regarding captive breeding of Snow Leopards, some zoos, particularly Helsinkis' and Chicago Lincoln Park, showed good success. The Padmaja Naidu Himalayan Zoological Park in Darjeeling is dedicated to the conservation of endangered fauna and started work on captive breeding project of this threatened mammal in the year 1983. It was selected as an ideal site for this captive breeding project. It was actually the first instance of an Asian Zoo participating in the Snow Leopard master plan conceptualized by Mrs. Helen Freeman, President of the International Snow Leopard Trust and also Species Coordinator of the 'Species Survival Plan' for Snow Leopards. The site selected for off-display conservation breeding centre of Snow Leopard was the north-western corner of the Birch Hill within the compound of the zoological park at an altitude of 6900 ft. On 21st March 1986, a pair of unrelated Snow Leopards was brought to Darjeeling from Zurich Zoo. Another pair was brought to this zoo from the US Zoos on 16.01.1989. This pair gave birth to two female cubs on 20.05.1989. This was the first successful breeding of Snow Leopards in the Darjeeling Zoo.

In the last two decades, there were 40 births of Snow Leopards in the captive conditions of the Padmaja Naidu Himalayan Zoological Park. Special attention was given to these species and all record-keeping of this programme as well as about the animals are done not only in, but also recorded with the International Stud Book Keeper of the species at Helsenki. Next plan of this project is to have at least few stable captive populations of Snow Leopards at Gangtok, Nainital, Shimla and Srinagar before reintroducing them in the wild. Darjeeling Zoo, till date, has around 189 Snow Leopards which is undoubtedly one of the largest captive populations of this species in a single zoo. The Snow Leopard Breeding Project at Padmaja Naidu Himalayan Zoological Park is one of the most successful and the only captive breeding programme of this species in South-east Asia.

Project Red Panda

The Project Red Panda in India evolved after a survey of Red Pandas housed in the Indian zoos in the year 1990. The result of this survey showed that there were very few Red Pandas in the Indian Zoos. The animals recorded were either very old or not kept in pairs and all the animals reported at that time were females. Experts suggested to introduce captive breeding activities in the Indian zoos and subsequently suggested to bring a male panda in the Darjeeling zoo for the three females present there. Darjeeling zoo was selected for the captive breeding programme of the Red Pandas for a number of reasons:

1. Darjeeling zoo had good facilities for Red Pandas;
2. It had maintained three healthy females in its collection for several years without any problems; and
3. These animals are indigenous to the region of Darjeeling and are, therefore, suitable from a climatic point of view.

This proposal was supported by recommendations of the global captive breeding programme (Glatson and Princee, 1993).

It was finally decided that a male belonging to the European Breeding Programme would be the first Red Panda to be sent to India. The prospects for breeding Red Pandas in Darjeeling looked promising. As the Red Panda breeding programme became successful, the problem of the surplus animals as well as the threat of inbreeding started to arise which gave birth to the idea of reintroduction of these captive animals in the wild. As a primary step of this reintroduction programme, locating a suitable site was of utmost importance considering several environmental and geographical parameters of the site, habitat preference and ecology of these lesser pandas. There were undoubtedly a number of suitable areas in eastern Nepal, eastern Sikkim, Bhutan and Arunachal Pradesh where such a project could be established. However, few of these had the added benefit of zoo support. Singhalila

National Park in Darjeeling district was later considered as a suitable site of reintroduction of Red Pandas in the wild (Glatson, 1993).

The Forest Department, Government of West Bengal, also took initiative in surveying areas in and around Darjeeling for Red Pandas and also to identify a suitable site for reintroduction of the Red Pandas in captivity.

Literature Consulted

Baillie, J. and Groombridge, B. (eds.) 1996. *1996 IUCN Red List of Threatened Animals.* IUCN, Gland, Switzerland.

Chaudhury, A., 1997. Red Panda *Ailurus fulgens* F. Cuvier in the North-east with an important record from the Garo hills. *J. Bombay Nat. Hist. Soc.* 92 (1): 63-66.

Caughley, G. and Gunn, A. 1996. *Conservation Biology in Theory and Practice.* Blackwell Science, Cambridge, Massachusetts, USA. Pp. 459.

CITES. 1983. *Identification manual. Vol.1. Mammalia.* Secretariat of the Convention of International Trade in Endangered Species of Wild Fauna and Flora. Gland, Switzerland.

Duckworth, J.W., Timmins, R.J., Khounboline, K., Salter, R.E. and Davidson, P. 1999. Large mammals. In: J.W. Duckworth, R.E. Salter and K. Khounboline (eds.). *Wildlife in Lao PDR: 1999 Status Report.* IUCN, WCS and CPAWM. Vientiane, Laos. Pp: 161-220.

Ellerman, J.R. and Morrison-Scott, T.C.S. 1966. *Checklist of Palaearctic and Indian Mammals, 1758 to 1946.* (2nd Edn.). British Museum (Natural History), London, England. Pp. 810.

Fox, Michael W. 1984. *The Whistling Hunters: Field Studies of the Asiatic Wild Dog* (1st Edn.). State University of New York Press, Albany, New York. Pp.150.

Gee, E.P. 1964. *The Wildlife of India.* Collins, London, UK. Pp. 262.

Glatston, A.R. (ed.) 1994. *The Red Panda, Olingos, Coatis, Raccoons, and their Relatives: Status survey and conservation action plan for Procyonids and Ailurids.* IUCN/SSC Mustelid, Viverrid, and Procyonid Specialist Group. IUCN/SSC, Gland, Switzerland. Pp. 103.

Glatston, A.R. and Princée, F.P.G.1993. *A Global Masterplan for the Captive Breeding of the Red Panda. Ailurus fulgens fulgens.* (Part 1). The Royal Rotterdam Zoological and Botanical Gardens, Netherlands.

Groombridge, B. (ed.) 1994. *1994 IUCN Red List of Threatened Animals.* IUCN, Gland, Switzerland.

Hilton-Taylor, C. (ed.). 2000. *2000 IUCN Red List of Threatened Species.* IUCN, Gland, Switzerland and Cambridge, UK.

IUCN 1972. *Red Data Book 1972. (Vol.1). Mammalia.* IUCN, Morges, Switzerland.

IUCN Conservation Monitoring Centre. 1986. *1986 IUCN Red List of Threatened Animals.* IUCN, Gland, Switzerland and Cambridge, UK.

IUCN Conservation Monitoring Centre. 1988. *1988 IUCN Red List of Threatened Animals.* IUCN, Gland, Switzerland and Cambridge, UK.

IUCN. 1990. *1990 IUCN Red List of Threatened Animals.* IUCN, Gland, Switzerland and Cambridge, UK.

Johnsingh, A.J.T. 1985. Distribution and status of dhole *Cuon alpinus* Pallas, 1811 in South Asia. *Mammalia* 49:203-208.

Kakati, K. 1996. *Survey of the Red Panda in Eagle Nest Wildlife Sanctuary, Arunachal Pradesh–a report.* Wildlife Institute of India, Dehradun.

Khajuria, H. and Sinha, N.K. 1986. Limiting factors in the population dynamics of vanishing Central Indian swamp deer *Cervus duvauceli branderi* (Pocock). *Wildlife wealth of India: (Resources and Management).* Majupuria, T.C. (ed.) Tec Press Service, Bangkok, Thailand. Pp. 479-491.

Molur, S. and Walker, S. (eds.) 1998. Conservation assessment and management plan (C.A.M.P.) workshop. Mammals of India report summary, *Zoos' Print.* Zoo Outreach Organisation, India. 13(9).

Mukherjee, S.K. 1994. Red Panda in Eagle Nest. *WII Newsletter. (April–June 1994). Special Issue on Himalaya).* Pp 29–30.

Myanmar Forest Department. 2003. *A national tiger action plan for Myanmar.* Ministry of Forestry and Wildlife Conservation Society. Yangon, Myanmar.

Nowak, R.M. (ed.) 1999. *Walkers Mammals of the World.* (6th Edn.). The Johns Hopkins University Press, Baltimore and London.

Panwar, H. S. and Gopal, R. 1984. Conservation of wild cats in India: The Plight of the Cats. *Proceedings of the Meeting and Workshop of the IUCN / SSP Cat Specialist Group.* IUCN, Madhya Pradesh, India. Pp. 63-80.

Pradhan, S. 1999. Observations of the red panda (*Ailurus fulgens*) in the Singhalila Park, Darjeeling, India. *Small Carn. Cons.* 21.

Pradhan, S., Saha, G.K. and Khan, J.A. 2001. Ecology of the red panda *Ailurus fulgens* in the Singhalila National Park, Darjeeling, India. *Biological Conservation.* 98 (1):11-18.

Rishi, V. 2003. Law and Wildlife Conservation. *The Wildlife (Protection) Act, 1972 (as amended upto 2003).* Natraj Publishers, Dehradun. Pp. 13–17.

Rodgers, W.A. and Panwar, H.S. 1988. *Planning a wildlife protected area network in India (Vol.1)*. FAO, Wildlife Institute of India. Dehradun. India.

Schaller, C.B. and Simon, N.B. 1970. The endangered large mammals of South Asia. *IUCN. 11th Tech. Meeting. (Vol.2). Problems of Threatened Species.* IUCN. Pp. 11–23.

Shackleton, D. M. (ed.) 1997. *Wild Sheep and Goats and Their Relatives. Status Survey and Conservation Action Plan for Caprinae.* IUCN / SSC Caprinae Specialist Group. IUCN, Gland, Switzerland.

Sinha, B.C. 2001. *Book on State Animals, Birds, Trees and Flowers of India.* Wildlife Institute of India, Dehradun, India. Pp. 1–39.

Valdez, R. 1982. *The Wild Sheep of the World.* WildSheep and Goat International, Mesilla, New Mexico.

Valdez, R., Nadler, C.F. and Bunch, I.D. 1978. Evolution of wild sheep in Iran. *Evolution.* Lawrence, Kans. 32: 56–72.

Won Chong Man and Smith, K.G. 1999. History and current status of mammals of the Korean peninsula. *Mammal Review.* 29:3-33.

Wynter-Blyth, M. A. 1956. The lion census of 1955. *J. Bombay Nat. Hist. Soc.* 53(4):527-536.

Yonzon, P.B., 1989. *Ecology and Conservation of Red Pandas in the Nepal Himalayas.* PhD dissertation, University of Maine, Orono, USA. Pp. 159.

http://www.animalinfo.org

http://animaldiversity.ummz.umich.edu

http://www.unep-wcmc.org

http://www.iucnredlist.org

http://www.cites.org

http://www.wii.gov.in

http://projecttiger.nic.in

http://envfor.nic.in

Index